W9-BRY-205

The Zen Path
through Depression

 HarperSanFrancisco
A Division of HarperCollins*Publishers*

The Zen Path
through
Depression

Philip Martin

HarperSanFrancisco and the author, in association with The Basic Foundation, a not-for-profit organization whose primary mission is reforestation, will facilitate the planting of two trees for every one tree used in the manufacture of this book.

A TREE CLAUSE BOOK

HarperCollins books may be purchased for educational, business, or sales promotional use. For information please write: Special Markets Department, HarperCollins Publishers, 10 East 53rd Street, New York, NY 10022.

HarperCollins Web Site: http://www.harpercollins.com

HarperCollins®, 📖®, HarperSanFrancisco™, and A TREE CLAUSE BOOK® are trademarks of HarperCollins Publishers Inc.

Book design by Ralph Fowler

FIRST EDITION

Library of Congress Cataloging-in-Publication Data
Martin, Philip
The Zen path through depression / Philip Martin.—1st ed.
Includes bibliographical references.
ISBN 0-06-065445-7 (cloth)
ISBN 0-06-065446-5 (pbk.)
1. Spiritual life—Zen Buddhism.   2. Depression, Mental—Religious aspects—
Zen Buddhism.   3. Zen Buddhism—Psychology.
BQ9288.M36   1999
294.3'4442—dc21   98-44251

99   00   01   02   03   ❖ RRD(H)   10   9   8   7   6   5   4

This book is for all those in my life who have taught me,
but especially for Dainin Katagiri Roshi, with deepest gratitude.

Contents

Acknowledgments

I am indebted to Scott Edelstein, first editor, agent, and friend. Without his patient, generous assistance and encouragement, this book would never have come into being.

Sally Colemier, who shared in the early presentation of these ideas, taught me about honesty and fearlessness in saying what I had to say and kept me mindful of why I was writing.

Myron Malecha, John Robertson, David Pfeffer, and Marie Boehlke helped me on my own path through depression.

My Thursday friends Pat, Nelson, Dewey, Fred, and Kelly shared my excitement and kept me sane.

Ted Pirsig, so many Friday mornings ago, helped me to rediscover the joy of writing.

Those people and families I worked with through the years courageously showed me, day in and day out, how to live with dignity and hope.

My coworkers through the years taught me much about compassion and the passion to help others.

John Loudon, Karen Levine, and everyone else at Harper San Francisco were a pleasure to work with. They understood the work, as well as the neuroses, of a first-time author.

I am grateful to all those who shared their own struggles and healing.

Dainin Katagiri, Tomoe Katagiri, and everyone at the Minnesota Zen Meditation Center were invaluable teachers on the path. Charlie Greenman and George Zanmiller were there to help when I stumbled.

Thanks to my mother and father for their support and love.

Above all thanks to Therese and Joe, for your love and patience. Therese, you have taught me so much about faith and courage, as you have made your own journey.

Introduction

In the middle of the path through life,
I suddenly found myself in a dark wood.

DANTE, *DIVINE COMEDY*

When I was seventeen, I went on a canoe trip with two friends in the wilderness of northern Ontario. We were on our own, with little more than our canoes and some dried rations. None of us were experienced travelers.

We thought we could do the trip without any help, relying on nothing more than our own resourcefulness and some good maps. But five days into the trip, we found ourselves utterly lost. We looked to our maps and we backtracked over our path, but still the landmarks we expected were nowhere to be found. A long rapids and waterfall were not where they were supposed to be, and there seemed to be a lake where one shouldn't have been. We were lost in unfamiliar territory, and our maps, and all the other resources we depended on within ourselves, were useless.

When at thirty-seven I found myself in a severe depression, the experience was much like being on that camping trip. I was again lost in unfamiliar territory, in a frightening yet beautiful place. All the landmarks were gone. Obstacles suddenly appeared where they shouldn't have been. The maps I had come to depend on showed nothing of the territory in which I found myself. Worst of all, I didn't even know myself that I was lost. And if I didn't know, how could anyone else know or offer help?

I had always depended on my practice of Buddhism to help me in difficult situations. But in this case it didn't seem enough, or relevant to what I was going through. Depression had stolen the life out of all I had found life-giving, and spiritual practice was no exception. Yet there seemed to be little that religious or spiritual teachings had to say about the experience of depression.

That isn't surprising, given the fact that so much of spirituality is based on the idea of transcendence and escape. And if there is one thing depression is not about, it is transcendence. It is instead an experience of being stuck in the mud, unable to rise up through the muck like the lotus flower so often used as a metaphor in spiritual teaching.

But I had always believed in a spiritual practice that was about settling deeply into life, going into the depths if necessary. So I persisted, trying to find a way to connect this practice to what was happening with me. Ultimately I discovered that in the downward movement of depression I could settle more fully into my life, and that in that settling there was great opportunity for learning, opening, and growing.

My practice and path are Zen Buddhism. I found I was finally able to bring my depression into the vastness of my practice, and I learned that others can, too—whatever their own spiritual leanings.

Depression is an illness not just of the body and mind, but also of the heart. Depression offers us an opportunity to deepen our spirit, our lives, and our hearts. There is much that we can learn about ourselves and our world through this journey. Through attentive, compassionate practice with the depression, it is possible to experience an even deeper healing, and grow in our spiritual lives.

This book is a guide to the wilderness that is depression, written by someone who knows the territory and has seen that a map alone is not enough. It is a guide to using our own inner resources, and to learning how to read and listen to the signs around us. It is ultimately a guide to growth, insight, and realization.

There is a story about Buddha in which one of his students asks him a highly speculative, theoretical question. Buddha responds with a story of a man who has been shot with a poisoned arrow.

Buddha then asks, "Would this man say, 'I will not allow this arrow to be removed until I know from what tribe the man who shot it came, or from what family he came, or what he did for a living, or what wood was used in the shaft'? In the same way I have not answered those who want to know is the universe finite or infinite, is there a God or not, or other such questions. And what have I revealed? The cause of suffering and the path to its relief."

It is in this spirit that I make the offering of this book, in the hope of giving practical help to others in the pain of depression. May you use this book to guide you through that pain, and perhaps through the greater suffering of this life we all share.

A Note on the Explorations

The explorations you will find at the end of the chapters are opportunities for you to more deeply investigate the ideas in the chapter. They are not something to feel guilty about not doing, or failing to do "right." Use them if they resonate with you—if not, move on. They are invitations, not prescriptions.

Most of the meditations and visualizations are based on traditional Zen and Buddhist practices. You may find they work best for you if you do them in a quiet place, sitting straight-backed on a cushion or in a chair, but again, use them in a way that works best for you.

The verses are based on traditional practice poems called *gathas*. Rather than prayers or affirmations, they are used to bring us back to the present moment, and to help us remember how we want to live when faced with an obstacle or opportunity.

The other explorations are also for you to take or leave, as you see fit. Be gentle with yourself. Remember, this is your path to walk, and you are the one to decide which way to take.

I wish you well on your journey.

Stopping to Listen

> When one needs to listen to a strange sound, doesn't one
> naturally stop making noise? One cannot listen carefully
> as long as one is talking, thinking, or moving about inat-
> tentively. The need to listen carefully creates its own still-
> ness. When one actually realizes how inattentive one is
> and begins to wonder about what is going on inside and
> out, doesn't one *have* to look and listen quietly?
>
> TONI PACKER

The gray place that depression is can be frightening and disorienting. Whether or not you have been there before, each time it is different. It may sometimes seem that you are in a cold, lifeless, lonely desert. Other times it may feel like a dark, overgrown forest, filled with terrible animals lurking just out of sight in the shadows. Or you may feel you're at the bottom of the ocean; the water holds you captive, the pressure is unbearable, and you cannot breathe. Whatever the place or the terrain, it feels as if there is no way out. You are truly lost.

When we are lost, frightened, or facing something new or unknown, our first impulse is usually to either run or fight. Years of evolution have built that into us. Though at times the moment calls for one of those responses, at other times running from our condition or fighting against it will only increase our pain and our sense of being trapped. Stumbling in fear and panic, we become more lost. In depression we often run until we become swallowed up in the darkness that has become our life. What may be crucial to our healing is, first, to do nothing.

This practice can be difficult, because it seems to go against all we believe. Yet to do nothing—to "sit down and shut up," as Katagiri Roshi would say—is the essential practice of Buddhism. Indeed, it was the experience of Buddha himself. He sat down under the Bodhi tree and vowed not to move until he had solved for himself the question he had been asking for many years.

This decision is often looked at as heroic, and when a person sees such a situation through to its end, it can be. But it is also an act of surrender, even an act of desperation. Buddha had already tried everything else in the world there was to try at that time. He had gone through the extremes of sensual pleasures, self-denial, and self-mortification. None of those paths had brought him the insight he sought. And so he decided to stop his seeking and just sit down.

There was in his decision a very real element of desperation, of his back being against the wall. There was also some curiosity in his decision. He wanted to find out what human life really was. Rather than study various philosophies and try to make them fit the circumstances he encountered, he made a study of himself. He vowed to unflinchingly face himself and his life and to see this deep investigation through to its end, wherever that led him. (That is what brings many of us to a spiritual path in the first place—a combination of desperation and curiosity.)

In depression our back is often against the wall. Indeed, nothing describes depression so well as that feeling of having nowhere to turn, nothing left to do. Yet such a place is incredibly ripe, filled with possibility. It gives us the opportunity to really pay attention and just see what happens. When we've done everything, when nothing we know and believe seems to fit, there is finally the opportunity to see things anew, to look differently at what has become stale and familiar to us. Sometimes, when our back is against the wall, the best thing we can do is to sit down and be quiet.

When we are lost in the woods, we can stop, look at our situation, and see where we are. And when we are in the midst of depression, we can stop and look at where we are and how we came to be here. We can look coolly and fearlessly at ourselves, our life, and our pain, without any thought of remedying them.

Zen Buddhists developed a method for working with the heart and mind in meditation through the use of what they called *koans*. Koans are often described as tools intended to shut down our thinking so that we can experience something deeper within ourselves. The word *koan* comes from a Chinese term that refers to a public proclamation or royal message. Koans give us a strong taste of our everyday mind, as well as a glimpse of what enlightened mind is.

Depression also comes to us as a royal message. In stopping and listening to depression, we can hear the message it brings. Zen Master Dogen's best-known writing is the *Genjokoan,* or the "Koan of Everyday Life." Dogen felt that the very questions of daily life— Why are we born? Why must we suffer and die? Who are we? How shall we live in this moment?—provide all we need to help us find the freedom we seek.

Depression calls all of these questions more strongly into our lives. These questions, and the strong taste of pain and suffering that accompanies them, are the seeds of our freedom.

Although it is often painful and frightening to approach depression, we can do so. We can stand and not run. We can even allow it in and let ourselves learn what it has to tell us.

Buddha sought the fundamental basis of his life, faced it squarely, and named it. We can do the same with our depression. To do so is not to give in to depression, but rather to take the first step in healing our pain and suffering.

Depression is not just a step further along the continuum of grief and sadness. Anyone who has experienced it knows that it is qualitatively different from our everyday consciousness. Depression brings to us strong feelings of hopelessness, a sense of worthlessness, and a more insistent awareness of death. But before we seek solutions, we must look at the naked feelings themselves. Facing depression lets us look closely, for perhaps the first time, at the deepest problems and feelings in our life.

We have a fundamental choice. We can run from these feelings, which will only make them stronger. We can try to fit them into a framework of belief—either our own or someone else's. We can see depression in moral terms and believe that it is a sign of weakness. We can view it in medical terms and seek treatment with a physician. We can believe it is psychological and seek in our past for the answers.

Or, before seeking any concept or explanation, we can do as Buddha did and look at things as they are. We can look compassionately at what is happening to us in depression. We can examine ourselves without running, without fighting, without preconceptions, before any thought of a solution.

Further Exploration

In a quiet place, sit either cross-legged on a cushion, or in a straight-backed chair. Fold your hands in your lap, and allow your gaze to drop to a spot on the floor a few feet in front of you. Sit upright, with your spine comfortably settled into your hips, and tuck your chin in a bit. Now let your attention move from your head, through your neck, shoulders, and chest, to settle in your belly. Feel the rising and falling of your belly as you breathe in and out. If you wish, you may think "in" and "out" with your breathing.

Become aware of the space around you. Feel that this is your space, your ground, your home. You are like a pebble sinking down through a river to settle on the bottom, where the waves and currents can't touch you. Envision yourself sitting on a throne, or a mountaintop—anywhere that seems a powerful place to you. Say three times to yourself, "This is where I make my stand." You are immovable here. You are strong and safe in this spot. All fears, all grief, all pain can come and wash over and through you, and not wash you away.

Now come back again to your breath, following it in and out, as your belly rises and falls. Your breath is the anchor that is always there, that will hold you in this place. Become aware that this place where you sit is immense and extends into all directions. It is large enough to contain whatever you choose to invite in. Welcome your feelings of fear, your pain, your depression into this place. Tell the depression that it need not feel excluded from this place, that in this place it will receive understanding and compassion. Invite into this place as well any deities, or energies, that you wish. Especially those that give you strength—but also, if you would like, those that may bring you fear. Again come back to your breath, and feel the immensity of the place within which you sit like a mountain.

When you are ready to return, remind all those you have invited in that they are welcome to return again when you come back. Remind yourself that this place waits for you, at any time you wish it. Sit, enjoying this place you have created. Let your attention rise through your chest, shoulders, and neck, and slowly open your eyes.

Exploring the Territory

Stand still. The trees and bushes beside you are not lost.
Wherever you are is called Here. And you must treat it as a
powerful stranger, must ask permission to know it and be
known. The forest breathes. Listen.

NATIVE AMERICAN ELDER

When we stop running, we can begin to look at what is
happening with us. We may be terrified, but we can set aside our
fear for a moment. We can just explore the situation.

We may have had preconceptions about depression—but
we will find that these are of no use to us, because they are nothing
like the direct experience of depression itself.

In depression we are in a world we have never seen before.
We may feel that we are different from other people. It can seem as
though everyone is speaking a language we don't understand. Our
minds struggle to keep up with all that is happening around us.
Even the air and the light seem different from what we have known
before.

Depression is not merely a deeper experience of our normal emotions of sadness, suffering, or grief. Those emotions are of
course present. But depression is an experience entirely different, in
both body and mind, from anything we have known before.

We need to learn the lay of this land called depression, both
to help us find our way out, and to help us survive while we are
here. For the path out of here may be difficult, and may take us a
while to find.

So it makes sense for us to begin to get our bearings, and
explore this territory we find ourselves in.

Intense emotions are present in us: hopelessness, worthlessness, and a profound and unexplained sadness. We feel that we are all alone. Thoughts of death intrude into our consciousness. We may even be filled with thoughts of suicide.

Our mind feels as though it isn't working right. It is difficult for us to form thoughts, to speak, even to make simple decisions. We feel a mental exhaustion, and our memory often doesn't seem to work. There is a slowing of our body and mind. Yet at the same time there is a speeding up of that voice in our head, screaming terrible things about us and the rest of the world. Depression robs us of our attention and judgment at the very time when we need them most.

We also feel a physical exhaustion. We feel weighed down, as though we were moving through water, or in heavy gravity. We move slowly and often feel that, whatever it is we may want to do, it is not worth the effort we have to expend just to move. We may feel that all we want to do is sleep.

The world around us seems different, too. It is as though someone had slowly turned down the lights, until it is difficult to see. All around we see filth and decay, hopelessness and death. We are exquisitely attuned to the sadness in the world—both our own pain and the pain of others.

This place may feel as cold and lifeless as the moon, or as deadly and oppressive as a barren desert. Or it may be a dark, menacing, overgrown forest where we can't see any way out, or even know in which direction to turn. Or we may feel like we are on the bottom of the ocean, where no light can penetrate, we can't breathe, and the pressure bears down heavily on us.

Depression can come on slowly. It can be like the light fading at the end of the day: you scarcely notice it until suddenly you can't see your own hand in front of your face. Or it can be like walking in a mist: you don't notice how wet it is until suddenly you realize you're drenched to the bone.

But we have chosen not to run away, so we stay with all of this. We pay attention to our feelings and thoughts, as well as to our secondary reactions—our desire to run away, to forget about our pain. We choose to face our life squarely, with awareness and compassion.

Though depression is different for each of us, it has many elements that are common to all of us. These confirm that there is a physical process at work. Depression does seem to be an illness, a disease of both mind and body.

Depression is a spiritual illness as well. It interferes with our ability to pay attention to this wonderful present moment, to see the goodness in this moment, and to feel the hope of moments after this one. It makes the gift of being a living human being seem a curse.

Yet as we approach depression in a spiritual way—and with others' help—we can find healing not just for our mind and body, but for our suffering spirit.

Further Exploration

Sitting comfortably on a cushion or a chair, relax your breathing. Then begin to focus on your inhalations and exhalations.

When you have settled into your own natural rhythm of breathing, bring your awareness to your body. What sensations do you feel that seem to be a manifestation of your depression? How do you feel that's different from how you usually feel? Is there a heaviness throughout your body? Do you feel especially cold, or especially hot? Or do you instead feel numb?

Notice whether there is pain, and where it is located. Do you feel a tightness in your belly, or a pain in your chest? Or perhaps you feel a restlessness, and find it exceedingly difficult to sit still. Give your awareness to those feelings, but do not respond to them. Instead, try to simply continue sitting and breathing, while paying attention to those sensations.

Now take a moment to focus your attention on your thoughts. If you can, watch them come and go without becoming involved in their content. If you find that you have become involved, gently bring your attention back to simply observing your thoughts. Are there thoughts that you're not accustomed to having? Are you thinking about death, or are there thoughts of worthlessness or pointlessness? Are you preoccupied with worry, or fear, or bad things that you feel will happen? Do not try to stop those thoughts or push them away, but simply observe and note them.

Finally, give your attention to your feelings, and notice how they are intertwined with your thoughts. Are you feeling fear? Hopelessness? Anxiety? Despair? Anger? Sadness?

Bring your attention back full circle, and look again at your body. Are your feelings and thoughts connected to some of the physical sensations you noticed earlier? As you pay attention to each sensation, thought, and emotion, does it intensify, or does it quiet down?

When you feel you are ready to stop, bring your attention back to your breath for a moment, and notice whether your breathing has changed since you began.

You can do this exercise from time to time to check in with your feelings of depression. Or you can do it over several days to really get to know your depression well.

———————

Sitting quietly, give your attention to your breath flowing in and out.

Now imagine that your depression is a physical place. What is it like? Does it feel like being lost in a forest, or stuck on the bottom of the sea, or stranded in a desert? Or are you in a large, dark mansion? Or something else entirely?

Explore this place. Notice what the air smells like, how warm or cool it is. What sounds do you hear? Are there any other people in this place? How do you feel here—lost, alone, afraid, confused?

You can return to this place at any time to examine your depression and become more aware of what it is—and how it may have changed.

Pain

What now is the Noble Truth of Suffering? Birth is suffering; aging is suffering; dying is suffering; sorrow, distress,
pain, grief, and despair are suffering; to not get what one
desires is suffering; existence with attachment is suffering.

BUDDHA

To perceive is to suffer.

ARISTOTLE

Students of meditation sometimes have trouble with pain
when they sit in the same position for long periods. The advice
many teachers give them is to make the pain the object of their
meditation.

In depression we also may be overcome with pain. It
screams for our attention. We grow so tired of feeling pain that we
will find nearly any way we can to avoid it. Sometimes we become
so tangled up in our pain that all of our energy goes to fighting it.

Often we aren't even aware that this is what's happening.
And when we respond in this way, we don't even really experience
the pain, because we are running so fast to get away from it. Sometimes we become so accustomed to trying to ignore it that we may
continue running even when the pain is gone.

Yet we can make pain the object of our attention, rather
than a monster to flee from. We can begin by going beyond merely
seeing it as "pain." We can examine the qualities of the pain, notice
how it really feels. We can notice if the sensation in our body is one
of heat, or tension, or pins and needles. We can notice whether we
have tightened up around the pain, or if our whole body is on edge
as we try to escape from it.

Then we can look more broadly at the ways we respond mentally. We may try to think of something else. Or we may tense up in the area around the pain—though this serves only to block it, hold it in, and magnify it.

After Buddha discovered the path of freedom, he began to teach others a way to find the same path. He described four fundamental truths about human life and death. The starting point for each of these truths is pain.

The first truth Buddha spoke of is that all of life is characterized by *duhkha*. This Sanskrit word is most often translated as "suffering." More accurately, it refers to dissatisfaction, to the fact that we live in a world where we all must deal with physical and emotional pain. Furthermore, when we experience pleasure, we must deal with the pain of worry—worry that the pleasure will end, or be taken from us.

Buddha made a distinction between pain and suffering. This is a distinction we seldom make. Simple uncomplicated pain is something we cannot avoid. The word *duhkha* refers to all the ways in which we complicate our pain through our rush to avoid it—and all the ways in which we make ourselves suffer as a result.

In depression we experience intense pain that is both physical and mental. We also frequently complicate that pain through our attempts to get away from it. And often we are unaware of just how much we are suffering, because we are so involved in trying to outrun our pain, or ignore it, or cover it up with anger.

Early in my own depression, I tried to deny what I was going through. People tried to tell me what was obvious to everyone else. It was finally my three-year-old son who woke me up to what was happening with me. He looked at me with loving eyes, and asked, "Daddy, are you not happy?" With that simple question, finally all my resistance began to melt away, and I could begin to look at how right he was.

When we stop running from our depression, we can begin to examine our pain, and give loving attention to ourselves and to it. We become scientists of our own pain, and notice where it resides. It is almost surely physical. It may be a coolness, or a tightness in our chest, or a piercing pain in our heart.

Though it is at first frightening to examine our pain, once we have done so we can begin to soften to it, and really feel our suffering. We may worry that the feeling is too intense, that we won't be able to stand it. But ultimately we find that the pain we feel in trying to avoid what is happening is at least as bad as the uncomplicated pain beneath it, if not worse. And we may find, to our surprise, that the pain underneath becomes more bearable.

As we notice our pain, we also begin to see how we respond to it. We may tighten around it, or armor ourselves against it, until this armoring becomes a way of life in itself. In this way, depression creates a barrier between ourselves and our life.

But when we can soften to our pain, and fear it less, we may find that we can begin to let the world back in again.

Further Exploration

Once you are sitting comfortably, focusing on your breath, bring your attention to any pain or discomfort you may feel. You may choose either physical or mental pain (the two usually don't exist apart from each other anyway).

As the pain begins to grow, remind yourself of your intention not to run from it, but instead to explore it thoroughly. When you first become aware of it, identify it as simply "pain." Then move on to look closely at its qualities. Where in your body is it located? Does it remain constant, or does it increase and then decrease? Is it a sensation of cold or warmth; of tightness, or numbness, or pins and needles? Is it an ache or a burn?

What happens to your pain when you pay attention to it in this way? Does it lessen? Increase? Does it seem less like pain and more like discomfort?

Now look at the thoughts that arise along with the pain. Do you think the pain should not be happening? Are you feeling frightened or angry? Do you try to move a bit in order to lessen the pain? Does this help, or does the pain quickly return? Do you tighten in the area around the pain? Does your breathing become shallower or more rapid?

Try to relax into the pain. If you are tightening around it, or your breathing has changed, allow the muscles to relax and your breathing to slow. If possible, allow your thoughts to ease as well.

What happens to the pain when you relax? What happens when you try to push it away, or avoid it, or change it?

If you can remain with the pain, you may be able to see that, without your doing anything, it ebbs and flows, arising and disappearing like thoughts or other sensations. Does this surprise you when it happens? Have you ever noticed this with anything else?

Impermanence

Think of this fleeting life . . . like a bubble rising in a
stream, a falling star, a phantom, a dream.

THE DIAMOND SUTRA

To renounce things is not to give them up. It is to
acknowledge that all things go away.

SHUNRYU SUZUKI ROSHI

Often in depression we are acutely aware of the fact that all
things are impermanent. Death, and thoughts of death sit heavily
on our minds. We think of our own death, and the deaths of all
those we care about and all things that matter to us. This can cause
us a great deal of pain—to know that all these things will end.

Though this awareness of impermanence is extremely painful, it is also an entry into a truth that Buddha saw as crucial to
explore: all things are impermanent. Or, to put it less elegantly,
everything put together falls apart. It is a truth many of us spend
our entire lives trying to ignore or forget.

I was painfully aware of this truth in my depression. It was
as though decay were a flower, and I saw it blooming in bursts of
impermanence all around me. It seemed to render all of my actions
useless and hopeless, as there seemed no point to any of them when
all the people and things we experience do not continue on.

But the world as a whole *does* continue on after us, and we
try to make it a better place for our having been here. Still, it is hard
to get past the feeling that in this world of impermanence, nothing
matters, and this sense can be especially strong in depression.

To try to make sense of this—or to do anything in the midst

of it—can seem, as Katagiri Roshi said, "like washing a clod of dirt in muddy water." But, he added, "still our practice is to go on, right in the midst of this hopelessness."

It is impermanence, Buddha said, that causes much of our suffering. Or, to be more exact, not the impermanence itself, but our refusal to see and accept it. Our suffering comes from our attachment to people and things, our repeated attempts to find something lasting where there is nothing lasting to be found.

We want to have the things that give us pleasure remain as they are. Indeed, we want our very selves to remain constant. But this truth of impermanence tells us not only that nothing lasts forever, but that nothing remains the same. The world around us, and we ourselves, are changing from moment to moment. Death is nothing but a more drastic change in a world where everything is changing anyway.

We would like to feel that we stand on solid ground, that there is constancy, certainty, and permanence that can support us. But if we choose to try to depend on such constancy, we are left standing on air. We are like the coyote in the old cartoons who runs off the edge of the cliff and suddenly finds that there is nothing under his feet.

A Zen koan recommends: "Standing atop a hundred-foot pole, take one step forward." Impermanence is that hundred-foot pole. Or, rather, our attachment and desire for permanence is the hundred-foot pole we remain tethered to, afraid to move. It is what keeps our lives small and confined, no larger than the top on our pole.

There is another way. We can step forward into that world of impermanence. Who knows? Rather than falling, we may find a new freedom. We may fall into the beauty of impermanence.

Every gardener knows that it is the very impermanence of the blossoms that makes them precious. The beauty of the garden lies in its constantly changing nature, in the waves of colors and shapes that are constantly moving through it.

The beauty of the world lies in the same constant movement. We can step into this beauty, into the midst of all that is dying and being born around us.

Further Exploration

Sitting quietly, focus on your breathing. Be aware of the rising of your belly at the beginning of each new breath, and watch as your belly falls as the breath ends, dissolving into nothingness. Be aware of this cycle—of beginning, of ending, and of new breath arising in its place.

Now turn your attention to your thoughts. Allow them to enter your mind and leave of their own accord, without your becoming involved with them or pushing them out. Be aware of how they arise and dissolve, only to have new ones arise in their place. Note this cycle of beginning, ending, and arising of new thoughts.

Now be aware of your bodily sensations. Notice how pain or restlessness or itching arises and dissolves, just as your breath does. The pain in your knees, if you don't become involved with it and attempt to get rid of it, will of its own accord arise and dissolve. As it leaves, new sensations—pain in your shoulder, an itch on your nose—will arise to take its place. Be aware of this cycle of beginning, ending, and arising of new bodily sensations.

Spend some time reflecting on impermanence in your own life. Think of the things or people that you thought would be with you forever but are now gone.

What other people and things in your life would you like to have last? Can you see that they too will, at some point in the future, no longer be with you?

Consider the cycle of beginning, ending, and arising again of people, circumstances, and things in your life. How do you feel as you think about this? Do you feel sad, or angry, or despairing? Do you have the thought that it is better not to get attached to anything or anyone because everything leaves?

Think of the time-lapse films of flowers blooming, in explosions of color, only to shrivel and die, and then to be quickly replaced by new blossoms. Can you imagine your life in the same way? Can you see how you too are part of this cycle of beginning, ending, and arising again?

Death

People think that only others will die.
They forget that sooner or later they will, too. . . .
Make the one word "death" master in your heart,
observing it and letting go of everything else.

SUZUKI SHOSAN

Buddha called death one of the main forms of suffering. He was referring not just to the physical act of dying, but also to the leaving of this life, with all its pleasures and joys, its relationships and attachments. We don't know what happens to us after death, but just the thought that we will no longer exist as we have in this world is terrifying.

An awareness of death reminds us of the precious nature of life, and thus provides us with a saner perspective on the problems of the life we are living. Nevertheless, such an awareness does not lessen our fear of the fact that we will die.

In depression we are keenly aware of death. Indeed, the thought of death seems to always be present in our minds. We may think about our own death often. At times we may even wish for it. We also think about the deaths of all the people and possessions and relationships we hold dear. We become acutely aware of the impermanence of all things around us.

And our perception is correct. This world *is* impermanent. Everything is living and dying around us constantly.

There is a story of a woman during Buddha's time whose child had died. She came with the child to Buddha, asking if he could bring the child back to life. Buddha responded that he could do so if she could bring him a mustard seed from a family that had not known the death of a parent, child, or friend. She went eagerly looking for the mustard seed. When she returned, empty-handed, she had learned that there is no one who is not affected by death.

We are not imagining it when we see death everywhere in our depression. Our task is not to lose heart over this and—most important—not to give in to the allure death may hold for us. It is our task to continue to live with an open heart, to live in this moment, with faith and courage.

We are all surprised when we read a story about two people who fall in love and marry even though one is terminally ill. It seems to require great love and courage to risk such a frightening and painful journey, to decide to love someone whom you know will be taken from you soon.

Yet isn't that what all of our lives are? We go forward, even though we too are here only for a short time. We live day after day, and love other fragile human beings with a tenuous hold on life. Doesn't this require great courage and great love?

Living in the midst of death is actually quite wondrous. Joseph Goldstein tells the story of a nun he met in India, who went out and dug a spoonful of earth each day. He asked her what she was doing, and she replied that it was a task her teacher had given her: "Each day, I dig a little more of my own grave." And Stephen Levine tells of a teacher who explained why he could fully appreciate the teacup he drank from. "To me this teacup is already broken," he said.

These stories may seem chilling, but they are of great value. Buddhist literature—and the literature of other religions as well—is full of stories of people who began searching for answers to the great questions of life after an encounter with death. The Buddha himself began his own spiritual search after watching a corpse being taken to its final resting place. So we could say that in depression we are fortunate, because we have a chance to taste death, to practice impermanence, to see death clearly for what it is.

The reality of death is a painful truth. It is what gives life its bittersweet taste, its mystery. But this is how things are, and for a time in depression we get to see without the blinders we usually wear. We have the chance to make a conscious choice—much like the person who marries someone who is dying. Though life will end in death for us, and for everyone, we can jump into this world and live in it fully. We can keep in our minds and hearts the awareness that death and impermanence are what give life its preciousness, its beauty.

An ancient Buddhist story tells of the great Tibetan teacher Marpa, whose oldest son had died. His students went to him and found him in great grief, sobbing and wailing. Shocked, they asked, "Teacher, how can you weep when you have taught us that all is impermanence and illusion?"

"Yes, it is true," he said, "and losing a child is the most painful illusion of all."

We are not seeking to no longer feel grief or sadness. Rather, we want to feel all that there is to feel, and to keep our hearts open in spite of the pain.

We love the world though all is dying around us. For all is being born around us as well. Depression gives us the opportunity to see this clearly. We can grieve for the losses, and we can delight in this world that is constantly re-creating itself, in flowers blooming and children being born.

Further Exploration

Sitting quietly, bring your attention to your breath. Feel the rise and fall of your belly as you breathe in and out.

Follow the inhalations and exhalations for a few minutes.

Now begin to focus on your breath as you breathe out. Feel the air going out and dissolving into the space around you. Notice the emptiness in your lungs and belly at the end of each breath. Focus on this space at the end of each outbreath. You may notice that your heart slows down during your outbreath, particularly at the very end. Notice too whether your thoughts and mind slow down at the end of the breath.

It has been said that awareness of the outbreath can be like a small taste of death. Give your full attention to each outbreath, as though it were your very last. Feel the breath and thoughts and energy leave you and dissolve into the air before you begin the process of living again as you breathe in once more. Now feel that moment when you have fully expelled all the air and your lungs and the rest of your body wait for the inbreath to begin. Continue to rest in that space at the end of each outbreath, and become comfortable and familiar with it. Could you be comfortable with this outbreath being your last?

What thoughts and feelings arise in you when you practice breathing and focusing in this way?

Now bring your attention back to the cycle of breathing in and breathing out. Notice the inbreath as an intentional act, continuing a cycle of life and death with each cycle of breath.

After you have watched your breath in this way, slowly bring yourself back to focus on things around you. When you feel ready, rise up from your seat.

Write your own probable obituary. How long did you live? What did you accomplish in your life? What did you fail to accomplish that you had hoped to do? What did people say about you at your funeral? Did you live a long life? Did you leave before you felt you were ready?

After you have finished writing, take some time to explore how this activity made you feel. Do you feel sad and angry? Is this the first time you have really thought in a concrete way about your own death?

In depression it is not only common but all too easy to think about suicide. We usually think either, "Everybody would be better off without me" or "Nobody would really miss me if I died anyway." Usually neither of these statements is true.

Take some time to think realistically about what effects your suicide would have on others. Imagine how the people in your life would actually feel if you took your life today. Imagine people finding your body, getting the news of your death. Picture them at your funeral.

Now look at these same friends, family members, and acquaintances in three months, in six months, and in two years. How do they feel about your being gone? What effect does it have on their lives? If you have children, how are their lives progressing without you? If you have a spouse or partner, what has happened to that person? Do you still leave a hole in the lives of your friends?

Now compare this picture with your image of no one missing you, or of others being better off without you. Is either of those images accurate?

Fear

For the wakeful one whose mind is unimpassioned,
whose thoughts are undisturbed, who has given up
both virtue and sin, there is no fear.

BUDDHA, *DHAMMAPADA*

Fear is a form of suffering, an anticipation of something bad to come. It is the worry that in some future moment we will not have what we want, or will lose what we have. We don't want to feel this pain. We don't even want to simply be uncomfortable.

Fear is a physical condition as much as it is an emotion. It tightens us up, keeps us from being relaxed and aware in the present. It colors our mind and our heart.

We are accustomed to having some fear in our lives. In fact, fear motivates much of our normal behavior. But in depression it seems that we are sometimes overcome with fear, to the point where we are almost unable to act. The fear may be so overpowering that it threatens to swallow us up.

Many of our usual fears are magnified in depression. We fear what others think of us. We fear that no one will love us. We are afraid of death. We are afraid of our own death. We feel that our depression and pain and fear will never end.

There are times when it is appropriate to feel fear: when a tornado is raging around us, when our car is skidding out of control, when our child is about to step into a busy street. When we are faced with real danger right now, fear is useful, and it is what we need to be feeling.

But much of our fear results from projection into the future—worry and anticipation over what might (or is going to) happen. In depression this psychological fear may overwhelm us.

Many people suffer panic attacks as part of depression. These attacks are essentially a fear of being afraid. We anticipate and imagine a frightening or uncomfortable situation and become afraid. Then we respond with fear and anxiety to the feeling of fear itself. Thus we create a vicious cycle of spiraling fear. This can continue to the point where we feel as if we are going to die.

The feelings and sensations of fear are very unpleasant, both physically and emotionally. Yet if, instead of running from our fear, or trying to push it away, we can open to and become aware of our feelings of fear and the thoughts surrounding them, we can stop the process of tightening up and constricting further. We can break the cycle of fear.

In depression stopping or slowing down the process of becoming afraid can be a great help. This is particularly the case when we are dealing not with a fear of anything in particular, but with that general feeling of fear and panic that sometimes arises.

In meditation, particularly in the early stages of practice, we may experience this same baseless but intense fear. As Katagiri Roshi has said, meditation can be like opening up Pandora's box. We remove the lid and let out the terrifying, ugly, and boring thoughts and emotions that we had locked away inside of us.

We must remember again our determination not to run. We can face these obstacles in our lives with compassionate attention. When fear comes up, whether in meditation or depression (or anywhere else), we can simply make it the object of our calm attention. We look at the fear; we see what it feels like. We notice if it is in our chest, our belly, or our throat. We note whether it is an ache or a tightness. We look at our response to this sensation. We see how the fear colors our thoughts and our emotions. We stay with it.

As much as we can, we stay present in the moment, for fear is generally a projection or anticipation of the future. But the reality is that this moment is the safest place to be.

A client I worked with had serious problems with panic and fear. Once, when he was in a strange place and beginning to panic, he called a friend and asked for help. The friend asked, "What street are you on? What color is the building across from you? What does the phone booth look like?" At first my client was angry, feeling that his friend was not helping him at all. But then he began to realize that his fear was receding into the background. What his wise friend had done was to bring him back into the present moment, away from the future and his fears about it.

In depression we have a chance to look at our fear for what it is. We can ask what being fearless might mean. And we can discover a fearlessness within us that will be available when we are in real danger. To be present with our fear, to meet it with compassionate attention, is to find this fearlessness.

Further Exploration

Sitting comfortably, begin to focus on your breathing.

After you have done this for a few minutes, begin to give your attention to your thoughts—the ones that make you feel afraid. Or simply bring your attention to any fear that is present in your mind.

Watch how your thinking is affected by this fear. Does it speed up? Do you have a desire to think about something else? Do you feel a sense of panic?

Don't try to talk yourself out of your fear; just allow it to be present, and continue to watch your reactions to it.

Now notice your physical sensations. What does fear feel like in your body? Where is it located? Do you feel a tightness in your belly or chest? Does your heart speed up, or your breathing become more shallow? Are these feelings unpleasant?

Don't try to change your reactions; just watch them.

Now come back to your thoughts and to the presence of the fear in your mind. As you watch it, does it increase? Or does it begin to lessen of its own accord when you simply allow it to be there? What happens if you notice yourself struggling against it?

Does the fear relate to anything that threatens you right now, at this very moment? Remind yourself that in the strength of your attention, in the solidity of your quiet sitting, nothing can hurt you right now.

Focus again on your breath and on the sensations in your body. Keep your focus there for several minutes.

After you have done this, is the fear still present? Is it as strong? Weaker? Even stronger?

Continuing to watch your breathing, remind yourself that you have been able to look at and examine your fear, and know that you have the capacity to do this again at any time.

Think of some things or situations you fear in your life, and pick one of the smaller ones. What might you do that would generate this fear in you? Talk to someone you are frightened of? Go someplace that scares you? Admit something about yourself to another person? Attempt something you've never done before?

Whatever this might be, resolve to do it, regardless of how you might feel about it.

Be aware of the nature of fear as anticipation. Are you thinking about what might happen, or what might go wrong, as you face this fear and move beyond it?

Do whatever it is you promised yourself you would do. As you do it, stop to notice your fear, anxiety, and anticipation. Remind yourself of your intention to complete the process and come out the other side.

Notice your breathing. (You may find that you are scarcely breathing at all!) Remind yourself that you are safe in your breath, in your calm attention, and in this moment. Take three or four deep breaths into your belly.

If you feel the urge to run, stop again to take several breaths and remind yourself of your intention to stay with the fear.

Consider this an experiment. If you were unable to finish it, or begin it at all, let that be all right, and acknowledge to yourself that you tried.

If you were able to complete this exploration, look at whether focusing on your breath and feelings in the moment may have helped. Compare your actual experience with what you feared or worried would happen. Were your fears justified, or did things go differently than you feared or expected?

As you faced your fear, did it threaten to take over, so that you became more afraid of the fear than of the specific situation itself?

Try this exercise with some more-imposing fears, and see what happens.

Doubt

This is not a simple doubt, mind you, but a "doubt-mass."
It is a doubt as to why we and the world should appear
so imperfect, so full of anxiety, strife, and suffering. . . .
It is a doubt that leaves us no rest.

HAKUUN YASUTANI

In depression we are acutely aware of the heavy doubt we carry within us. We doubt that things will ever get any better. We doubt ourselves because we can't easily make decisions. And when we do make a decision, we doubt whether it was the right one.

We second-guess ourselves constantly. We doubt whether any effort we make can come to any good. We doubt whether we can ever really know ourselves and our life. We doubt whether anyone else truly cares about us. At bottom we doubt God or the whole universe.

Obviously this is a very uncomfortable place to be. We would like to be able to dwell in certainty. We try to find that certainty in ourselves. Failing that, we try to find it in whatever person or thing outside of ourselves is available. We look to a job, a relationship, a belief, or a philosophy to give us that certainty. We want to feel that we know what our place is in the world. We want our life to be predictable and right.

Many people come to religion, including Zen and Buddhism, looking for that certainty. They hope that through religion they can have their doubts relieved. Some religions and teachers do offer assurances. They promise a certain and safe place in an uncertain and sometimes dangerous world.

But in depression all the reassuring and comfortable touchstones we had (or thought we had) in our lives are gone. We feel adrift, with nothing to believe in. The doubt within us sits heavily in the pits of our stomachs. We can't seem to get rid of it no matter how hard we try.

When our doubt grows big enough, we want to expel it, to get rid of it forever. We want certainty in its place. Failing that, we at least want to find something we can believe in.

Unpleasant as this place may feel at first, it is actually a very good place to be.

Though in looking for certainty we may initially turn to religions and teachers, the wisest teachers will encourage this doubt within us. Indeed, this doubt is itself a great opportunity and teacher.

Typically, we may look to religion or philosophy for some belief or explanation that can be a safe harbor in the storm. But in our life the storm rages on. There are no such safe harbors. There never have been.

Some of us who come to Buddhism may feel for a time like we have been conned in an enormous bait and switch. We have read some of the teaching and feel that it resonates for us; we hope it will give us some explanation, some anchor, something helpful to believe in. Instead, we are told to examine everything. We are encouraged to doubt. We are urged not to believe anything until it has been proven to us through our own direct experience.

Most Zen koans—questions and stories that Zen practitioners are often asked to meditate on—are meant to actually *increase* our doubt. The very first koan usually given, a koan simply called *mu,* has been likened to swallowing a hot iron ball that sticks in one's throat.

Hakuin, a great Zen teacher of the eighteenth century, taught that great doubt is one of the foundations of Zen practice. Often, doubt is what brings us to Zen teachings and meditation in the first place—doubt over who we are, why life is so painful, and how we should live knowing that we will die. We must then take this doubt, meditate with it, and digest it, until it fills our whole being.

We must become willing to reside in the midst of this enormous doubt and let it be all right. In fact, we must accept that it may never be resolved and that this will *still* be all right.

This means that we continually question; we never simply accept the answers others give us. It means that we do not hold on to the answers even when we have discovered them for ourselves.

If we can live with this doubt, we can then be continually ready to be surprised—by life, by ourselves, by our answers, by our experience.

My teacher, Katagiri Roshi, liked to say that we study something only to understand how little we know about it. To live in doubt is to live in mystery, to let mystery be large and vital in our lives. Human life is bigger than anything we can ever believe or understand about it.

This is why the doubt we are given in depression is a gift and a great teaching.

Further Exploration

A verse for when doubt arises:

> *When doubt springs up in my garden*
> *I will stop myself from pulling out the root*
> *And water this blossoming mystery*
> *with the manure of certainty.*

The Body's Grief

Often the wisdom of the body clarifies
the despair of the spirit.

MARION WOODMAN

This very body is Buddha.

HAKUIN

Most of the great spiritual traditions are in agreement that the body is finite. Though they differ in their views of the mind or soul, all agree that, in the end, the body will turn to dust. (It has been widely observed that the difference between human beings and animals is that human beings know they will die.)

Deep in our flesh, our bodies know they will die. They feel keenly the lost energy of old age, the taste of deterioration that is sickness. In our DNA we know this truth of impermanence. Our bodies grieve this loss, the preciousness and precariousness of life.

Depression is not only an experience in the mind; it is also an affliction of the body. There is a lack of energy, a painful heaviness, a sadness and a grief that permeate to our marrow. The sadness and grief we feel are, in part, the body's longing for permanence, for in everything it senses, it feels nothing but change and decay. When we can approach this grief and sadness without fear, there is the possibility of tapping into the grief of all the world, the suffering of all beings.

In depression we may feel grief all around us, hiding just below the surface on the faces of everyone we see. In seeing this, we become aware that all this pain comes from the same place. Then, when we cry, we cry the tears of the world.

In Buddhism the body is rightly perceived as the means through which we achieve enlightenment. Yet our technology aims increasingly at making the body obsolete. Today we often ignore one of our bodies' most basic needs, the need to be of use. We drive instead of walking. We get takeout instead of cooking. We throw our soiled dishes in a dishwasher. We shave quickly with an electric razor rather than feel the pleasure of a lather brush against our face, the weight of a razor in our hand.

These and other devices are sold to us with the promise of making a pleasure out of what was once drudgery. In fact, all they do is make these tasks faster; the tasks themselves remain neither pleasure nor drudgery. The real pleasure lies in the activity, in feeling mindfully the sensations of doing just that activity—in doing just what we are doing, so wholeheartedly, so fully, that the simple activity fills the whole universe.

In depression the sense of slowness and heaviness is like what you feel when doing walking meditation. In the extreme effort required to complete even the smallest action, such as waking up or walking across the room, lies the opportunity to experience and feel that action fully.

Thus we can take pleasure in the feeling of the warmth of the sun on our backs, or even the warmth of the lightbulb burning behind us. We can see how these feelings were lost to us before the depression, as we went through our busy days unmindful of our actions.

Depression gives us the chance to move back into our body, to feel all that we have been missing.

Further Explorations

Practice walking meditation. Find a quiet place with enough room to walk and turn around. Stand with your arms at your sides or clasped comfortably in front of you, your feet bare, and your eyes softly focused on the floor. Bring your attention first to your breath, feeling your belly rise and fall as you breathe in and out. Now let your attention move downward, noticing your posture and muscles as they hold you upright. Notice how all your body feels—shoulders, chest, belly, buttocks, and legs. Feel your weight resting on the soles of your feet. When you are ready, raise your right foot, heel first, as you breathe in. Be aware of your weight shifting to your left foot as your body moves forward. As you breathe out, set the ball of your right foot down. Notice as your weight shifts now to your right foot. As you breathe in again, begin to raise your left foot. Continue to walk slowly and methodically for as long as you are comfortable, giving full attention to the sensations of your entire body in the act of walking. When you are ready to stop, pause to feel the weight on the soles of both your feet as you stand still again. Move your attention fully to your breath once more and raise your eyes.

You can also practice this meditation informally when you are walking someplace, simply by focusing your attention inward, on the sensations of walking.

Pause throughout the day to notice the position of your body, whether you are standing, sitting, or lying down. Move your attention from your head to your toes. Notice the pressure against your body where it rests, whether your muscles are tensed or relaxed. Do parts of your body feel warm or cold? Be aware of your clothes against your skin, or of fresh air on bare skin. What is the sensation in your chest, or in your belly?

Prepare and eat a meal in silence. Appreciate the green of the broccoli, the heft of the knife in your hand, the smell as you slice through the potatoes. Listen to the bubbling of the simmering stew, and feel the warm steam as it rises and meets the cold spoon you are holding. Before you eat, give a silent thanks. Listen to the spoon scrape against the bowl, and smell the aroma of the food as you bring it to your mouth. As you eat, feel the warmth of the rice and the cool of the fruit, first on your tongue, then moving into your belly.

Don't stop there; wash the dishes with the same appreciation and mindfulness that you gave to cooking and eating the meal.

Desire

What is the truth of the origin of suffering? It is that
craving which gives rise to fresh rebirth, and bound up
with lust and greed, now here, now there, finds ever
fresh delight. It is the sensual craving, the craving for
existence, the craving for non-existence.

BUDDHA

Desire nothing, and you're content with everything.
Pursue things, and you're thwarted at every turn.

RYOKAN

Often in our depression we experience sensory overload.
We have lost some of our filtering abilities, and all the noise of the
world seems to be clamoring for our attention. We are assaulted by
sights, smells, sounds, and thoughts, and we feel there is no moment
of peace. Shopping in a crowded grocery store, riding the bus, or
just walking through the city can be too much for us. We are worn
out as our attention catches one sensation after another.

At the same time, moments of stillness and quiet may make
us uncomfortable as well. When we are alone with our emptiness
and pain, we yearn for stimulation to take our mind off of these
feelings. This can lead to almost compulsively seeking pleasurable
experiences to distract us.

In either state there is a stickiness to our senses. Like flypa-
per, they pull in and attach to everything they come in contact with.

The second fundamental truth Buddha described is that
the suffering in our lives is caused by our desire, by our grasping—

in particular, by our grasping for sensation. The Sanskrit word he used is *trishna,* which means "thirst" or "craving."

This thirst for experience, sensation, and pleasure is the cause of our suffering. Our suffering thus takes the form not just of pain, but of a psychological and existential dissatisfaction. It is the constant uneasy feeling that we should have more, that we should be happier than we are. We fear that the next moment could bring us more pain, and hope that it will bring us more happiness.

This desire keeps us wanting more and more sensation. In particular, it keeps us wanting pleasurable feelings. We attach to pleasure and avoid pain, and we try to avoid merely uncomfortable and neutral feelings as well. And even when we experience something pleasurable, it is flavored with the knowledge that we could lose it, so we attach to it even more strongly.

In our world of high-speed computers and constant stimulation, we feel at times that we cannot get away from the sensory assault. Yet rather than feeling that all of this stimulation is enough, we continue to want more—faster computers, brighter colors, new pleasures and experiences. This experience of dissatisfaction only leaves us desiring more, giving our thirst and clinging a desperate, addictive feeling.

It is not our experience of pain or pleasure that causes our suffering. Suffering is what we add to experience. The process of our attaching to pleasure and avoiding pain keeps us dissatisfied, and ultimately keeps us from being fully present in our own lives.

Depression, with its intensity of pain, allows us to see this grasping and avoidance. We try to avoid the pain we feel and cling ever more strongly and desperately to anything that might give us relief, or at least pleasure.

But we can begin to stop our chasing after pleasure. We can stop running from our pain. We can stop holding life—and ourselves—in our tight grip, and begin to truly experience our life. In seeing our grasping clearly for what it is, we can begin to change.

Further Exploration

What are the things that you believe you need to make you happy—that one more thing that will make you feel complete? What things do you turn to when you are feeling lonely, or sad, or grieving, to help you forget those feelings? Can you watch this impulse within you, to avoid pain and seek pleasure, and not give in to it? Is this difficult to do? How do you feel when you don't follow the desire?

———

One way to see our grasping and clinging is to look at our boredom. When you are alone, is it difficult not having anyone to talk with? When you are bored, do you feel anxious? Do you use the phone or the television or the radio just to relieve the boredom? What happens if you don't give in to the boredom, and instead just watch it?

———

Meditation is a place where we frequently find ourselves bored. When we sit quietly with few sensory or physical stimuli, it is easy to become bored and restless.

Watch this boredom when it comes up. Do you look for something to occupy or entertain you? How do you do that?

Perhaps you think of pleasant memories from the past, or worry about the future. You may think about stories you have read, or songs you like. Or you may just fantasize about sex, food, or other pleasures.

Don't judge these impulses toward pleasure when you are bored. Watch your reaction to the boredom. Where does the boredom originate? Does it feel uncomfortable? Is there an element of grasping in your wish not to be bored, but pleasantly entertained instead?

What happens if you don't give in to the boredom, but just watch it?

Escapes

What we can't face looks for us anyway.

JOHN TRUDELL

A Zen monk should even waste time with
wholehearted attention.

ZEN SAYING

One of the hallmarks of depression is a loss of interest in things that used to bring us pleasure. These include not only music, movies, hobbies, and friends, but more fundamental activities such as eating, sleeping, and sex. The world has gone gray, and the sun gives no warmth.

In Buddhism there are three types of sensation: pleasurable, unpleasant, and neutral. In depression it seems that all sensations fall into the realms of unpleasant and neutral.

In such a situation we try to find something to give us pleasure. Or, if we can't find pleasure, we at least hope to escape from what is painful into the realm of the neutral. Yet the pain that we are running from seems to wait for us in every moment.

In our ever more desperate efforts to soothe ourselves, we turn to drugs, alcohol, or overindulgence in food, sex, or work. When those don't help, we may turn to some of our newer toys— television, computers, video games. Or we may look to religion with the same desperation and greediness of mind.

Of course, the efficacy of all of these is always quite limited. This is even more true than usual in the bleakness of depression. Yet most of us only try harder with the same solution, or bounce from one to another. Still, the pain is always there waiting for us.

As with many other features of depression, this response is a magnification of our normal consciousness and life. It is a more severe case of our tendency to run from what is painful in our lives, to avoid pain at all cost.

Much of human life—and many human activities—are dedicated to this quest. In the realm of depression, however, we are presented with the opportunity to examine the quest more closely. Partly this is because the pain is more intense, but mostly it is because we are so unsuccessful in escaping depression in this way.

Most of us run from pain of all types. This reaction keeps us from being fully present in our lives, from fully feeling joy as well as pain. Our escapes thus keep our lives at arm's length, and we are left with the vague, uncomfortable sense that something is not right, that something is missing from us and our lives.

Depression takes away this luxury of turning away from our own lives. We cannot outrun our uncomfortable feelings anymore. This gives us the opportunity to see how we do turn away, and how this reflexive flight simply does not work. Finally, when our backs are against the wall, we have an opportunity to change. When there is no escape, we can find a new freedom.

First, though, it is necessary to look at two misunderstandings that cause us to run. The first is that there is something wrong with being in pain. To be in pain simply means to be alive, to be a feeling human being. Buddha pointed out that once we are born, we suffer, feel pain, grow sick, and ultimately die.

Of course it is natural to avoid pain. Avoiding pain keeps us alive. To leave your hand in a flame would be foolish. But this is not where we make our mistake. We go wrong when we believe that we should not feel pain—that this current painful moment, this current experience, should not be. We believe there is another right moment in which there is no pain.

When we believe that this moment in which we feel pain should not be, or is somehow wrong, we may then begin to believe that there is something wrong with us. Or else we look for something outside of us, something wrong with this world, to blame for this pain. This thinking is our second misunderstanding, and many of our problems follow from it.

When we see the situation as our suffering selves on one side, and the problem causing that suffering on the other, there appears to be no other choice but to act upon the world outside of us to make ourselves happy. Carried to the extreme, this belief becomes addiction or compulsion, as the addicted person tries repeatedly, even though without success, to find peace in the single answer he or she has chosen. This common, futile belief is simply part of the human condition, which Buddha and others have described.

The attempt to solve problems through what is outside of us leads to much of human activity. In spiritual practice there is the chance to see the faultiness of this logic, which most of us have built our lives upon.

The real obstacle in turning back to ourselves in depression is that we have the feeling there is something very wrong at the very root of ourselves, that we are deeply flawed. Anything that turns us back toward ourselves, that forces us to conclude that we have a part in creating our unhappiness, seems only to confirm this view.

Depression is often thought of as a disease of self-centeredness. While it is true that in depression we may be more concerned and involved with this self than usual, that is only because the self seems so flawed and worthless. At first even admitting the fact of the depression is difficult, because to do so seems tantamount to admitting that our view of ourselves as broken is correct. Instead, we may go on for years blaming others or the world. For many, the initial acceptance of the depression thus itself becomes the great barrier. But if we can forget these ideas of right and wrong, of responsibility and blame, true healing can begin.

In dealing with the pain of depression—or of being alive —it is necessary first to accept the pain and to stop trying to run from it. Its origins, causes, and solutions are not as important as our acceptance of it and our intimacy with it.

Meditation gives us a great opportunity to do this. In making a commitment to a meditation practice, we also commit ourselves to try not to run from the pain, but instead to explore and investigate it.

When we investigate, we begin to see how we judge our pain, and how we react to it. We may become angry, or fantasize, or look for someone to blame. Soon we can see that these attempts to avoid the pain don't work. If we persevere, we find that we can survive our pain and finally come to a place of peace and joy, even while the pain is still there. In fact, the pain becomes a part of this peace.

If we accept the pain of our depression, and investigate it, we can see our attempts to escape for what they are. Then, as we begin to experience the pain more fully, joy also appears.

Soon we begin to understand the distinction between pain and suffering: pain cannot be avoided, but the suffering that comes from our attempt to avoid pain is not necessary. As my Zen teacher, Katagiri Roshi, often told us, "All you have to do is stand up straight in the midst of your suffering."

Further Exploration

Identify one of the things you use to escape when things aren't as you want them to be—food, television, sex, work. For an hour, a day, or a week, choose not to turn to your personal escape when your life becomes too painful—not in order to feel virtuous but as an experiment, simply to observe this process. And if you do begin that activity, stop and watch. Notice how you are feeling when you turn to that escape. What is the painful feeling like? Is it physical, emotional, or mental? How do you feel when you can't use your escape? Do you try to find something else to use in its place? How long does the feeling last? How do you feel when the desire to escape has passed?

Now go ahead and allow yourself the escape when you want to turn to it. But again, notice how you feel at the moment you want to escape. Pay attention to how you feel as you do the activity. What triggers your desire for this diversion from uncomfortable feelings? How long do you participate in the activity? Why do you decide to stop? How do you feel after you've given in and escaped for a while? Is the painful feeling still there? Is it less strong?

Picking and Choosing

The Great Way is not difficult. Simply avoid
picking and choosing.

JOSHU

A hair's breadth of difference, and heaven
and earth are set far apart.

SENG-TS'AN

One of the main characteristics of my own depression was
the cynical and judgmental state of mind it created. In public I was
constantly looking around at other people, mentally judging them
on their clothing, their manner, their speech. I had a difficult time
reading, because as I read I heard myself criticizing the author, thinking I could write much better, or make a better argument. I imagined that the people I was close to lived their lives out of highly
negative motives and thoughts.

My judgments about myself were even more severe. I constantly upbraided myself for my every thought or action. I felt that at
the very bottom I was defective, a shiny red apple rotting at its core.

I already had some experience and knowledge of what Buddhism calls the discriminating or judging mind, but in my depression it was as if that mind had been given a megaphone. I became
aware of how this discriminating mind is constantly in the background, attempting every moment to affect how we live our lives.

Depression brings this judging mind out of the shadows
and allows us to see how present it is in our thinking. Though it
may be louder and more negative in depression, it can also be positive in its judgments. At these times it may be harder to see. But
positive judgments can create as much of a problem for us as nega-

tive ones, for we are still busy picking, choosing, judging, evaluating, and categorizing.

Our discriminating mind examines each experience and determines whether it is pleasant or unpleasant, then determines whether it should be sought or avoided. It compares and groups everything we come in contact with. We consider how something is like other things we have experienced and how it ranks and compares with all the others.

This discriminating mind is indispensable for many activities in our life. It has been said that it may be the cause of much of our suffering, but it sure helps when you want to catch a bus. The difficulty is that we don't know when to listen to it and when to treat it like a fussy child—kindly, but firmly.

Our picking and choosing ultimately keeps us from experiencing our life. We are often busy making up our minds about an experience rather than meeting it intimately, with an open mind. As we consider all things, assessing and ordering them, we ignore the reality of their interconnectedness.

Jesus said, "Judge not, lest you be judged." This is not just a description of cause and effect. Depression allows us to see that through the judgments we make of others and ourselves, we create much of our own suffering. When we judge and discriminate, in that moment we ourselves are judged, because we must live in this world of judgments that we have created.

Further Exploration

During quiet meditation, after you have settled in to sitting and are watching your breath, move your awareness to your thinking. Step back and observe your own thoughts. This may be difficult at first, but each time you notice that you have become involved in thinking again, simply return, without self-judgment, to observing.

Pay particular attention to the way you mentally judge and organize. Do not try to stop this judging. When you become aware you are doing it, simply note to yourself, "Judging."

Our judging, discriminating mind is subtle. You may find that you are judging yourself: "I'm such a terrible person for being so judgmental" or "I'm a bad meditator because I can't do this." When you find you are judging yourself, simply note it. It may even be helpful to think, "Oh, here comes judging again" as a way to reduce the attached blame.

When you feel you are done, return to your breath for a few minutes before you stop.

In your everyday activities, bring your awareness to your thinking, and note when you are judging. Again, don't blame yourself. Just note, "Oh, judging again."

To experiment with how judgments may affect you, try doing some things you have always believed you hated. Listen to country-and-western music, read a detective novel, rent a Sylvester Stallone movie, or watch an evangelist on television. Approach the activity with an open mind, and pay attention to your thinking. Note when and how you are judging throughout the experience. What did you feel as you did this? Were you disgusted? Surprised that you enjoyed it? Did the judgments you made allow you to feel superior?

To see how judgments affect your relationships with other people, identify a person you dislike intensely, or have strong judgments about. Then, for one week, make an effort to set your strong feelings aside. Try to imagine what that person's life is like. Without the person knowing it, do something kind for him or her: leave the person a piece of candy, send a friendly but anonymous postcard, do some work he or she is expected to do.

How do you feel about this person during this time? While you are doing something nice for him or her? At the end of the week?

Does he or she behave differently toward you? What do you believe about yourself now that you have done this? Were you a "bad" person before? Do you judge yourself with pride after being kind for a week? Is either of these judgments correct? Does it matter whether it is right or wrong?

Anger

A Zen student came to Bankei and complained, "Master,
I have an ungovernable temper. How can I cure it?" "You
have something very strange. Let me see it," replied
Bankei. "Just now I cannot show it to you," the student
replied. "When can you show it to me?" Bankei asked. "It
arises unexpectedly," explained the student. "Then,"
concluded Bankei, "it must not be your own true nature.
If it were, you could show it to me at any time. When you
were born you did not have it, and your parents did not
give it to you. Think that over."

ZEN STORY

In depression we may feel literally sick with anger—anger
at ourselves for being stuck in depression, anger at the depression itself, anger at those who can't help us or don't seem to understand.
Or we may be filled with an anger that seems to be free-floating, un-
attached to any particular thing or thought.

At times anger may be our predominant feeling in depression. Sometimes this is simply the nature of our particular depression. But it may be that we don't consider sadness and grief to be
acceptable emotions, so instead we allow ourselves to feel only
anger.

In Buddhist teachings, anger is considered one of the "three
poisons," along with greed and delusion about who we really are. In
depression anger does seem to poison our body and mind—yet we
seem unable to affect or control it.

Depression allows us to see anger in its bare condition, and
to see how we are both repulsed by and drawn to it. We may be

drawn to it as a replacement for the sadness we feel, and as an anti-dote to our sense of hopelessness and powerlessness.

Anger strengthens our sense of a self—a self that we feel is important and must be protected. Most of our anger flows from this self, especially when we feel that it is being threatened or ignored. Examining the thoughts and emotions that underlie our anger can tell us where the anger begins. This can help to lessen anger's hold on us.

But before we look at what lies underneath it, it is helpful to look at the raw anger itself. When we look dispassionately at anger, we see that there is an energizing quality to it. When we are angry, though we feel uncomfortable, we may also feel empowered. Here is where anger's attraction can lie, especially when, in our depression, we are feeling powerless and insignificant. Anger can overcome our feelings of fear and sadness, can create heat where there seems to be no life.

So there are two problems with anger: we can feel uncomfortable with it, and may try to run from it; yet we may also feel drawn to it, and may try to keep its heat burning.

Little good comes from indulging anger. Anger colors all of our thoughts and feelings and perpetuates ways of responding that cause us pain. Anger can also cause us to lash out and harm others.

We will find, though, that if we try to eradicate anger, we only meet it with more anger. Then our anger naturally builds rather than dissipates.

We have another choice, however. We can meet our anger with loving attention, as we might the anger of a small child, to see past it and find what is under it. Rather than trying to kill the anger, we can approach it with nonviolence and love.

We can begin with an awareness of when anger is present, and how it affects our thoughts and actions. When we look at anger calmly and directly, we take away its underpinnings, so it doesn't remain for a long time, but rather arises and disappears without our attaching to it. We allow our anger to come and go, rather than grabbing it, turning it over and over, and building it up by pouring gasoline on its fire.

It is in attaching to our anger that the difficulty arises for us. Shunryu Suzuki Roshi once said about meditation, "You can let your thoughts come into your mind—just don't invite them to stay for tea." We can do the same with our anger. We can let it come and go, but not create an environment where it feels encouraged to stay. We can deal compassionately with the underlying fear that we feel. We can also take the energy of the anger, which is probably something we desperately need in depression, and direct it toward positive action for healing.

Anger can be like a dowsing rod, leading us to our fears, but also to situations that may require our action. It is not always baseless. It does not need to be avoided or pushed away or branded as useless. Rather, it can provide us with the energy, the resolve, and the clarity to respond appropriately to whatever situation we may find ourselves in.

Further Exploration

Sit quietly, watching your breath.

Begin watching your thoughts. If angry thoughts are present, identify them as anger, and watch them without interfering with them.

As the anger is present, what happens to your thinking? Do thoughts come faster, or does your mind feel agitated?

What are the sensations in your body with anger present? Does your breathing speed up, or become more shallow? Do you feel heat or cold anywhere in your body? Does your heart speed up or feel irregular? Is there a tightening anywhere in your body?

How do you feel about this anger? What are the thoughts and sensations that accompany it? Do you feel uncomfortable? Energized? Do you feel an impulse to get involved in the anger and keep it going? Or do you want to be rid of it? Just watch your reactions, without following through on them.

What happens to the anger if you can just observe it? Does it remain? Grow stronger? Or does it fade away?

Focus again on your breath. As you watch your breathing, what happens to the anger? What happens to the sensations in your body? Continue for as long as you feel comfortable.

Stop to pause in the middle of anger, and rest in your breath for a moment. Look particularly at your thoughts. What thoughts give rise to the anger?

Can you look at or interpret the situation in a different way? Does doing so change your anger?

Do you have a desire to remain angry? How does it feel if you change the intensity of your reaction? Can you put your energy into responding to the situation in a way other than being angry?

Time

Because the signs of time's coming and going are obvious, people do not doubt it. Although they do not doubt it, they do not understand it. See each thing in this entire world as a moment of time. Things do not hinder one another, just as moments do not hinder one another.

DOGEN, *UJI*

In the midst of depression, time has a different quality to it. Movement, speech, and thought all slow down. (In fact, this "psychomotor slowing" is one of the formal psychological criteria for diagnosing depression.) It is difficult to perform physical tasks, due to the slowness and heaviness that fill the body. This can be a real problem if you're driving, or watching a child, or trying to hurry to an appointment.

In depression it begins to become clear that the "normal" world is based on speed and aggressiveness. We can also see that this is only one of many possible views of time.

In working with men and women with mental illness, I have watched many people go through a manic episode. When in a manic state, a person is filled with great energy and often euphoria. They speak rapidly, dream great dreams, require very little sleep, and have enormous physical energy. They can be quite engaging. (Some manic people are successful businesspeople and politicians.) The difficulty in helping them lies in the fact that they don't see that there is any problem. Often, others around them don't either. One woman I worked with used to say, "If I could bottle this manic energy and sell it, I'd be a millionaire."

Our very culture is manic, mimicking all the qualities of a manic person. Indeed, these qualities are widely admired and desired. ("I wish *I* had your energy, your enthusiasm, your drive.") As a culture we measure time by the nanosecond, distance between locations means nothing, and achievement is all-important. It's no wonder, then, that in depression we feel ashamed and useless, and believe that we must quickly do something to remedy our glaringly out-of-sync condition.

Yet the slowing down in depression gives us an opportunity to explore the world. It can be like the experience of a meditation retreat, where we have time to simply be, without reference to time.

In depression we find that the speed of time is not constant, as we are accustomed to thinking it is. Often it goes by slowly because of the uncomfortable feelings we experience. When we are in pain, or bored, or unhappy, we try to lean into the future, hoping we can hurry things along to a happier moment. (This is the basic human response to suffering or discomfort.) I think of my six-year-old son, feeling he couldn't wait for his birthday to arrive. He began to cross off days on his calendar before they arrived, as though he could move time along faster that way. We do much the same thing ourselves; we are just less obvious about it.

Trying to lean into the future in fact magnifies the discomfort and pain we feel in the present moment. It adds an extra layer of suffering to the pain. This can only be so, for we cannot get rid of the emotional pain we may feel right now. We can add to the pain, however, by wishing or hoping that things were otherwise. Dogen said, "In spite of our love, flowers die, and in spite of our hatred, weeds bloom."

Of all the things we experience, which do we have less control over than time? Whether it is moving slowly or quickly, we cannot force it to be any different than it is right now. We cannot get rid of it or reverse its direction. And we can be sure that time, as well as our circumstances, will change. In fact, that is the *only* thing we can be sure of. The pain we are feeling now will open into the next moment—into new pain perhaps, or into joy.

Time is like the waves on a lake. The waves arise over and over again. Each is different, and the way they appear just ten feet down the shore can be completely different from how they are right here. Their arising each moment is dependent on innumerable factors. Sometimes they come slowly, sometimes quickly. They may be huge, or they may be the merest ripples. But my desire for them to be any certain way is lost in the immense sound of them breaking on the shore. So it is with the moments that arise around us.

This observation is familiar to anyone who has had the experience of returning from a long meditation retreat back to the frantic urban world. It becomes starkly apparent that the pace of life is not absolute, and that the speed we spend most of our waking hours moving at is manufactured. We don't have to move at that pace at all times.

There is value in moving slowly, as depression forces us to do. We can open to the moments unfolding around us. If we are attentive, we find there is time to do all that each moment calls us to do.

In the martial art of aikido, there is a practice called *randori,* in which a person deals with a great number of attackers all at once. But students quickly learn that they are not really dealing with many at once, that the only way to get through the exercise is to attend to one attack or attacker at a time. Get ahead of yourself by even a second by worrying about what is coming next, and you are lost, away from the moment. In the same way, we must deal with each moment as it presents itself, like a single pearl on a great string of pearls. Then we can find the beauty within each moment.

Further Exploration

Put away your wristwatch and other clocks for a few days. Pay attention to the flow of time within you. When does time move quickly?

When does it seem to move slowly? What are your thoughts and feelings at those times? If you aren't paying attention as closely to "real time" outside of you, is there even an awareness of time's speed? If you do become aware of how fast real time is passing, how does that speed compare with your own experience of time? What seem to be your natural rhythms?

Drive ten miles per hour slower today. What does it feel like when you don't feel the imperative to speed this current moment along? How do others seem to respond to you? How do you feel about this difference?

A Larger Meadow

To give your sheep or cow a large, spacious
meadow is the way to control him.

SHUNRYU SUZUKI ROSHI

In depression our life often feels out of our control. We feel
hopeless, as though there is little we can do to make things better.
But at the same time, most of us believe that we can change what
happens to us.

As we move deeper into depression, we try harder and
harder to find ways to overcome it. Being unable to effect much
change, we feel more and more that there is something wrong with
us. We feel we *should* be able to overcome our depression—if not
through strength of will, or affirmations, or positive thinking, then
at least through getting help from others.

But despite all of our best efforts, there are times when depression simply does not improve, or improves only slightly. And
when the improvements we had hoped for don't occur, we feel all
the more hopeless and worthless.

Depression brings us face-to-face with the fact that there
are many things we don't have control over, no matter how hard we
may try. Certainly there are many things outside of us that we can't
control; but neither can we control much about ourselves. We can't
will ourselves to grow a foot taller, or never get sick, or stop losing
our hair. And we will die no matter how healthy our diets are or
how much we exercise.

We live in a time in which control is prized above all else.
Our heroes are people who have achieved success, riches, and power
—all forms of control. Even New Age thought, which claims to

draw upon much ancient wisdom, is to a great degree about power and control. The axiom that "we make our own reality," and the belief that we can have anything we want if we only envision it, both stem from the same basic desire for control.

The great spiritual traditions speak instead of the wisdom of realizing our true place in the world. A deepening spirituality is not the result of more and more control, but of a greater and greater acceptance of our inherent powerlessness.

In our depression we can start to heal by accepting that a great part of our becoming depressed, as well as much of getting over it, may not be within our control. In doing so, we can let ourselves off the hook, and stop taking the blame.

We can then see that becoming more realistic about our power and place in this world, and seeing how little of it we really can control, are actually a deepening of our wisdom. We may even find that we have times of greater happiness and purpose when we simply relax, let go of control, and open into the moment. At such times we can take all that we are given as a gift.

At its most basic, our wanting to control our world stems from our attachment to pleasure and avoidance of pain. It is another form of *duhkha,* of suffering, of our complicating, and adding to, our basic experience. Control often means resisting the way things are, or believing they should be different. We then decide that we are the one to change them.

As our attachment to having things a certain way lessens, and as we let go of our belief that our life should go in a certain direction, we can also let go of our desire to control. We can then become a participant in our life, rather than the frustrated would-be director.

When we stop trying so hard to control those things we can't control, we also save ourselves a great deal of effort and energy—two things that are critical to maintaining our sanity and equilibrium in our depression. Rather than trying to affect things we have little control over, we can focus on the things that truly *will* make a difference, for us and for others.

In trying to control everything, we make our world smaller. Instead, we can open into a larger world where we are not in charge, but are a part of something much larger—something deeply wondrous.

An End to Suffering

What is the Noble Truth of the extinction of suffering?
It is the complete fading away and extinction of this
craving, its forsaking and giving up, liberation and
detachment from it.

BUDDHA

When we are depressed, we may feel as though we have always been depressed and will always be depressed. We seem to be stuck in pain and suffering, and we see no possibility of an end to it. Even seeing the ways in which we run from our suffering and chase after pleasure to cover up our pain seems to bring little change.

But the possibility of an end to our suffering is real. The heaviness we feel in depression can lighten. The oppressive heat can give way to a cool breeze, as a hot summer day gives way to the evening. This heat can be relieved through the cool breath of understanding.

The third fundamental truth Buddha taught is that an end to suffering is possible. Through understanding the ways in which suffering arises, we can stop creating more suffering.

The end of suffering comes through the cessation of our greediness, our grasping, our clinging—much as an addict stops using a drug. We stop this clinging and extinguish our thirst not by drinking some magic spiritual elixir, but by seeing for ourselves how our thirst arises.

The way to end our suffering is to loosen the tight grasp we have on life, to stop searching so hard for pleasure. We no longer seek newer, greater, more intense experiences. Instead, we just let our life be what it is—and in doing so we can, at last, *experience* it for what it is. And as we loosen our grip, we can begin to see the end of our suffering.

There may be much fear behind taking this new step, for it is contrary to what we usually do. We want to reassert our control and hold on tight again. But in order to stop our suffering, we have to allow pain into our life. Surprisingly, when we do, we will begin to reduce the suffering we create in response to our pain.

This solution is not complicated, though it is by no means easy to carry out. But when we know that the possibility of ending our suffering does exist, when we can feel the cooling breath, we can set ourselves on the path that leads to a new way of being and living. For most of us this will be a slow process, but it will be one that can help to heal our depression. We can move out of the suffering and fear we feel weighing upon us. The process also offers us the possibility of a satisfied, joyful life, whether we are depressed or not—a life where our circumstances are not what matters.

We no longer need to feel that we are not enough, and that we don't have enough. For perhaps the first time in our lives, we can feel that we do have everything we need.

My Zen teacher said that this process is not extraordinary. It is like finding a comfortable room to spend the night in at the end of a long journey.

That place is there waiting for all of us. It always has been there. All we have to do is stop our seeking and grasping for the answers.

Further Exploration

Examine your beliefs about suffering. Do you believe it is inevitable? Or that it builds character? Is suffering connected with struggle for you? Would there be no life without suffering?

Can you see a distinction between pain and suffering? Is it possible to have pain without suffering? Can you imagine a life without suffering?

The Truth of Joy

Let us live most happily, possessing nothing;
let us feed on joy like radiant gods.

BUDDHA, *DHAMMAPADA*

When I was younger, I developed a philosophy that I thought would shield me from pain in my life. It is a variation on what many of us try to do. I called mine the Outward Bound approach to life. Like the people in those solo survival exercises, outfitted only with a fishing line, a safety pin, and a match, I resolved to make it through life entirely on my own. I would depend on nothing and no one except myself.

Though there is great value in being self-sufficient, it seems to me now that I made no place for joy in my life. My goal was only to avoid suffering. But life is more than just survival and the avoidance of pain.

Many times in the darkness and desperation of depression, we would settle for just getting rid of our intense pain. Occasionally we do have periods of feeling nothing—neither happiness nor sorrow. Clearly, those are better than the periods of intense sadness, doubt, and fear. But there is little or no joy in our life.

Some people unfamiliar with Buddhism see it as a dry, joyless spiritual path that leads to a similar kind of neutral ground: the end of suffering. The Buddha's teachings arose in the midst of Hinduism, which saw life as intense suffering and little else, and in comparison it may have seemed that what Buddhism had to offer was at least better than a life of pain.

Yet, far from being a dry, joyless, intellectual exercise in casting off pain, the path that Buddha offered is one of turning toward and moving into joy. While Buddhist practices do point us toward the cessation of *duhkha,* or suffering, they also direct us toward *sukha,* or joy. Rather than a dry desert, we can find a forest rich with life, filled with plants, animals, rushing rivers, and cool springs.

It can sometimes be hard to believe this when we are in the midst of the intense pain of depression, yet it is helpful to remember that our goal is to move away from pain and death, toward joy and life. We too can find a life where we don't just survive.

When my depression was at its worst, and I realized I needed some kind of help, I finally went to see our family physician. I had known him for 12 years, through all the usual ailments. It was just after New Year's, and I told him I had been feeling irritable, despondent, tired, hopeless, and worthless.

He looked at me and said, "You must have been a ball to have around over the holidays." I laughed for the first time in months. I saw for a short moment the possibility I could accept my depression and even let go of it. Even in the midst of that pain, I could laugh.

Far from making our way through life with only a fishing line, a safety pin, and matches, we can find many tools and much help. We can have people whom we love and who love us. We can make use of all the tools available to us. Most important, we can find the joy and purpose that has always been there, for us to uncover.

Further Exploration

A verse to remember:

> *When suffering overwhelms me*
> *I will breathe in*
> *and leave an opening in this moment*
> *for the joy that lies just behind it.*

Freedom

All things are ultimately liberated.
There is nowhere that they abide.

GREAT TREASURE-HEAP SUTRA

If you can just observe what you are and
move with it, then you will find that it is
possible to go infinitely far.

JIDDHU KRISHNAMURTI

Depression can feel like imprisonment. When the world we see has become small, when everything seems dark, when we feel cut off from everyone, depression can even feel like solitary confinement. No matter what we do, we feel ever more incarcerated or oppressed.

We usually think of freedom as something opposed to imprisonment, and in that context we always see it as freedom *from* something—oppression, suffering, fear. We also believe that our imprisonment comes from outside of ourselves.

Yet our imprisonment—both in depression and in our everyday lives—comes instead from within. It is something we create rather than something imposed on us.

Since our isolation and confinement ultimately issue forth from ourselves, we are the ones with the power to free ourselves. We can find, even in our depression, not only a new joy but a new freedom.

This freedom does not come from having no limits. Instead, this freedom is the result of clearly *seeing* our limits, and our place in the world. We can then move into a greater interdependence with all beings and a greater responsibility to all beings. Within this interdependence, we are not confined by the limits of our small self. Here we can begin to find—and live in—a larger world outside of ourselves. And we can begin to let go of our need to have that world be a certain way.

When we are free from our habitual attachment to pleasure and avoidance of pain, we can find the joy available to us regardless of our circumstances.

As we leave behind our attachment, we can also begin to leave behind the pain of our depression. Our depression may still be present, but it no longer binds us to greater suffering and fear.

We have not even realized it, but we have been the jailer who has kept us imprisoned. We have lived within a small life, where we feel we are safe, and where we believe we can force our circumstances to comply with our desires.

We can give up on this attempt to force things to be the way we believe they should be. We can stop hiding in this cell where we feel safe—and in doing so we can leave our prison behind. Like an inmate coming out into the light and fresh air, we can find a larger and more spacious world. It is a world not limited by the confines of our suffering, not even by our ideas of freedom.

Seeing Without Blame

Drive all blames into oneself.

TIBETAN PRACTICE SAYING

When our life becomes painful, or seems not to be working, it is almost automatic for us to look for somewhere to place the
blame. This is not the same as examining our situation and remain-
ing open and curious.

Particularly if we are frightened or suffering, we jump right
over the step of examining the situation, and instead begin a frantic
search for someone or something to blame. We usually first look to
a source outside of us, since we don't want to accept the responsibility. It is our spouses, our children, or our friends who are responsible for the pain we feel. We soon become bitter and angry at the
whole world.

It is just as easy to choose to blame ourselves, since one
common symptom of depression is a sense of being defective at our
very center. We feel that we are to blame for all of our suffering. We
may even feel responsible for the problems and suffering of others.
At its worst, depression can cause us to feel that we are responsible
for all that is wrong with the world. Thus, our depression can seem
to confirm all of our worst fears about ourselves.

Either way, looking to place blame follows from our belief
that if we are in pain, something is wrong, and we feel we must find
a way to avoid the pain and the situation we find ourselves in.

Both actions push our pain away, and distract us from what
is really happening. For, whether we blame others or ourselves,
blame is a barrier to the true understanding of, and true intimacy
with, our lives.

There is a Zen story about a young monk who was working in the kitchen of a monastery. In picking vegetables for supper, he accidentally caught a snake, which he chopped up and put in the evening meal, utterly unaware of its presence. As he served the meal, the biggest piece of the snake ended up in the bowl of the master of the temple. Angry at finding meat in his bowl, the master bellowed, "What is this?" The young man looked at it, promptly ate it, and replied, "Thank you very much."

The action the young monk took in the story is often referred to as "eating the blame." Eating the blame means that we should take all of the blame into—not onto—ourselves. This story teaches us that, like the young monk, we can move beyond all blame, putting aside our desire to either place blame on others or take it all upon ourselves.

When we feel that our back is against the wall, blame is one method we use in trying to escape. Yet, although one common feature of depression is that feeling of being up against the wall, blame will not help us. A blind search for someone or something to blame can only leave us feeling more worthless, unsatisfied, and angry.

Instead, we can eat the blame by putting it aside, and look at *what* is, rather than *why* it is. We can stop trying to understand everything, and stop trying to escape from our feelings and our pain. Instead, we can come back to the raw and painful act of just being with what is happening to us. And in doing so we discover once again that nothing is as horrible when we accept it as it seems when we are trying to run from it.

We usually look at our difficulties with an eye to understanding why things are, and anticipating that the answer will tell us what we need to do. Instead, we can look deeply and quietly, not seeking understanding. We can look out of a deep curiosity, just to see how things work. When we do this, we may find that there is nothing that needs to be done, and that just seeing things as they are is enough. Or we may find that an answer presents itself to us simply in our looking at the process.

This practice is so fundamental to Buddhism that the first type of meditation practiced by many Buddhists is called *vipassana,* or insight meditation. *Vipassana* is a form of seeing deeply into ourselves and this moment. The insight that this meditation yields can help us turn from suffering to joy.

This is what happened for Buddha on the night of his enlightenment. He saw deeply into the workings of his mind and body, deeply into his own nature.

If you have made an effort to look into yourself, into your depression, and into your suffering, then you too have learned many truths about yourself and your reactions. You are able to investigate this situation you find yourself in. You can continue to face fearlessly the bare facts of your depression and suffering. Perhaps, without even knowing it, you have changed yourself through this very act of looking. You have changed the depression through seeing it clearly.

When we can see our situation without looking for explanation, we can come to a deeper understanding, an understanding beyond our usual ways of thinking. Within such an understanding, solutions may be revealed to us. We learn to see what is truly effective, what works, and what may be making matters worse. We can then begin to take action and begin (or continue) to heal.

Further Exploration

When something goes wrong in your life, where do you look to find blame? Do you immediately start to take the blame on yourself? Do you go first to someone or something outside yourself? If you do look outside yourself, do you have favorite people or things you blame?

Be aware of your impulse to place blame when it comes up. Can you just watch it, setting aside the need to follow it? How do you feel when you do this?

Stay with the situation and the uncomfortable feelings you have. Do you want to find some way to take away those feelings?

Can you look at the situation without blaming or trying to find a solution? Is this difficult? Do you feel some relief at not having to find someone (or yourself) responsible?

Does waiting and simply observing the situation change it? Does anything need to be done? If action does need to be taken, do you find a different response than you usually would if you looked for blame?

———————

Whom do you blame for your depression? Yourself? Your family or friends? Your job? Your life? God?

Does blaming help to relieve your depression? Or does it prevent you from taking action that could be helpful? Does blaming contribute to your anger or feelings of worthlessness in your depression?

Can you accept not knowing where your depression comes from? Does that feel uncomfortable? Or is that a relief in itself?

———————

A verse to use with blame:

> *When all goes wrong and I look for the blame*
> *I will eat that slippery morsel*
> *and look past the blame*
> *to see what really is.*

Breaking Open Your Heart

A person in pain is being spoken to by that part of himself
that knows only how to communicate this way.

MALIDOMA PATRICE SOMÉ

Depression is in many ways like suffering from a broken heart. Indeed, when you slow down and begin to pay closer attention to the depression, the physical symptoms themselves may often center in the chest. Anxiety is the fast-beating heart. Hopelessness is the tired heart. Sadness and grief are the pained heart.

In some systems of healing, illness is considered to be primarily a matter of imbalance. The symptoms point to the systems that are out of balance. In depression often the imbalance is between heart and mind.

For many of us in these times, mind and thought are considered to be useful and valued, while heart and emotions are seen as obstacles. We don't really know how to grieve and feel pain, but we definitely know how to think. That was true in my life before my depression.

In the experience of depression, this mind we have depended on so much fails us. It is difficult to make simple decisions, to remember small matters. We feel slow and stupid. Depression in fact magnifies many aspects of our personality and our thought process. Our mind becomes preoccupied with judgments and comparisons.

We can begin to see that this is not just the mind of depression, but to a great degree the nature of our everyday mind and thoughts. Indeed, our depression allows us to see this ever more clearly.

Meditation helps with this, as it can foster real detachment from these thoughts and moods. We can then begin to disentangle ourselves from our pain. We can begin to move away from what Zen teachers call small mind. We begin to be less impressed with our own thoughts.

As the grip of this small mind is lessened, the feelings and emotions of the heart are increased. For a person who has ignored the heart, its calling is persistent and unfamiliar. There are sadness and grief over the past, over all the fleeting moments behind us. We feel all the mistakes we have made, all the hurts we have caused. Depression can be a door into an exploration of our grief. This may be the first time we have faced our grief and honored it, rather than running from it.

Too often on the spiritual path we believe we should feel uncomfortable emotions less often, and that we should not attach to them. In acting on these beliefs, we may be casting those feelings away, or running from them.

But our hope is to practice compassion and kindness toward all. We must practice in this way toward ourselves and our own uncomfortable emotions as well.

It is one thing to be lost in our emotions, so that we become our anger or sadness. It is quite another to acknowledge, accept, and listen to them. In the strong and sometimes overwhelming sadness of depression lies the opportunity to face these difficult feelings with tenderness and compassion, rather than turning away from them.

Another new opportunity can be the experience of empathy. In the depths of depression, a woman I know found she could not watch television, because she wept at almost everything—even the long-distance telephone commercials where family members called just to say, "I love you." In my own depression, I would find myself fighting back tears at the grocery store just from seeing an older person struggling to carry his or her bags. Opening ourselves into the greater world, we may be feeling for the first time the grief of that world. In that feeling, we can find a compassion within ourselves that is as natural as breathing, a compassion that is always there.

My teacher said that too often we search for some grand and complicated conception of compassion. Yet it is as simple as pulling a child out of the path of a car. Compassion exists within us before any thought of compassion has formed in our mind.

In Buddhist terms this is the real experience of *duhkha*, suffering, and *annica*, impermanence. The experience of grief and sadness in depression can be our hearts calling us to listen to suffering and impermanence in our lives.

In learning how to see and honor these feelings of grief and suffering, we can find the compassion we have ignored for so long. It is not just a setting right of the imbalance between head and heart. If we honor this process, the initial feelings of being raw, vulnerable, and unprotected can break our hearts wide open. We can truly feel for the first time—feel not just the grief of our own mind and body, but the sadness of all beings in this world.

The open heart sees that there is nothing to protect itself against, that safety is an illusion. In this seeing lies true fearlessness. For as we may find when faced with a physical danger, sometimes the safest place to be is as close as possible to what we fear.

Further Exploration

Sit quietly and comfortably. After you have spent a few minutes watching your breath, bring your awareness to your chest. If you pay close attention, you can feel your heart beating. You may feel it slow down as you breathe in, and speed up as you breathe out. Notice whether it feels heavy, or quickened, or tight. Is this accompanied by a feeling such as grief, fear, or hopelessness? Do not push away the feelings. Meet them with warmth and compassion, as you might a lost child. Assure those feelings that you want to know them, that you will listen to what they have to tell you. You may want to speak to them of your grief and regret at having ignored them.

Bring thoughts of warmth and compassion to yourself as well. Remind yourself that there is no reason to feel shame over the things you may not have listened to. And that there is great courage in choosing to listen now, to let your heart speak. You may have felt as though there were steel bands around your heart, or that it was encased in crystal. See those bonds lessening, dissolving. Feel your heart opening, and know that it can do so slowly, at the pace it chooses. Let your heart grow, until its warmth and sure rhythm fill your whole body. Remember that there is nothing you need to steel your heart against, or protect it from.

Intense feelings may arise. This may happen the first time you practice this meditation, or after you have done it a few times. Let the sadness, grief, or joy wash over you and through you. If the feelings bring tears, shortness of breath, or laughter, let those come. Honor and embrace those feelings, again meeting them as you would a child, or a lost traveler. Let them know they are welcome and have found a home in your heart.

Once more send thoughts of warmth and compassion to yourself, for having the courage to listen to your heart. Feel the beating of your heart once again, and note how it follows with your breath. Bring your awareness to the rising and falling of your belly, to the anchor of your breath. When you are ready, raise your eyes and stand.

You Are Enough

All people have enough and to spare:
I alone appear to possess nothing.
What a fool I am! What a muddled mind I have!
All people are bright: I alone am dim.

LAO TZU, *TAO TE CHING*

We all know the feeling of being insufficient, of not being enough, of not mattering, of not deserving to be here on this planet.

Depression often engenders or accentuates those feelings. We are awash in a sense of worthlessness, convinced that we mean nothing to anyone. Those feelings can make it easier to take the next step of suicide, and leave this world that we feel we don't belong in, and that doesn't seem to want us anyway.

When we feel this way, the Buddhist teaching that we have everything we need, and that we are already perfect as we are, can be hard to swallow. To think that we are already Buddha, already enlightened, already who and where we need to be, seems a cruel joke. If this is so, why do we not *feel* enlightened? Why do we suffer? Why must we work to uncover this enlightenment?

Yet even in the midst of these feelings and questions, it is possible to find the seed of our awakening, the seed of our Buddha nature within. We see it in our not giving up, in seeking after truth, in offering our unhesitating help to a friend. Like a seed in the soil, this one is buried deep within us, far from light, and it needs nourishment in order to grow and come forth.

Meditation is one way of nourishing this seed. Other ways include laughter, and working with others, and making our best effort in each moment. Also acting in a way that acknowledges our connections with others, and the sacred nature of all beings.

In these times, and in this culture, it is not surprising that so many of us see ourselves as valueless. Many of us have been raised to believe in an innate sinfulness in each of us. In addition, in America we believe in the supremacy of the individual, that all of us can achieve anything we want to—and that if we don't, it is because there is something lacking in us. New Age thought further encourages us to think that everything that happens to us is due to our thoughts, dreams, and beliefs. And even American Buddhism has taken the concepts of karma and reincarnation and wrongly distilled them into a Buddhist Puritanism, where our joy or sorrow in the present moment is supposedly the result of whether we have been good or bad in the past.

Depression gives us the opportunity to see how strongly these feelings of being worthless, of not belonging, may lie at the bottom of our beliefs about ourselves. Yet simply seeing these beliefs directly for what they are, without fighting them, challenging them, or running from them, can help the feelings to dissolve.

We begin to do this when we simply let these feelings and beliefs be there with us, not driving them away. When we can let them become familiar to us, they are no longer monsters to be feared. Rather, many of the things that we feel make us unworthy—anger, greed, and fear—have simply been our all-too-human responses to pain and suffering.

As we begin to find new freedom in our lives, and a better understanding of who we are and what our lives actually are, we can also leave behind our feelings of unworthiness. We can exist, as Allen Ginsberg said, "without credentials . . . without apology." We can see that we do belong here, that we do carry the seeds of compassion and goodness within, that we are enough.

Further Exploration

Sitting comfortably on your chair or cushion, pay attention to your breath. As you breathe in, feel how you fill and grow in space. Let your belly grow large as you breathe in, and contract as you breathe out.

Take in the fresh air that the earth offers to all beings. Feel your physical substantiality as you sit there, filling up space like all other things around you. Notice how everything else around you exists with no apology, with no explanation of how or why it belongs there.

As your feelings of not being enough come up, let them arise—and when they begin to dissipate or weaken, let them go. Come back to the basic truth that in this moment you do exist.

Sit straight and tall, with the awareness that you are alive, that you matter, and that you can make a difference in the lives of others. Feel your kinship with all other beings in the world, and your basic right to exist, and to give and take from the world just as they do.

If feelings of pride come up, let those come and go as well. Accept that they too are part of who you are, but are not all of you. With kindness and acceptance, remind yourself that these are only part of what makes you human.

After you have settled in to your breathing, bring your attention to your heart. Feel the heaviness, the sadness that may be in it as it beats. Look into your heart and see all the ways you have been told that you are not enough, that you do not matter, that you don't belong here.

As you continue to focus on your breathing, see in your heart all the times you have told yourself you are not enough, that everyone else is better than you, that you don't measure up.

Look at the hurts you have stored there in your heart. The times when people told you that you were stupid, or worthless, or unimportant, and you believed them. The times you were hurt, or left behind, or left out. The times you weren't chosen, the times you didn't get to belong, the times you were alone and didn't want to be.

Yet as you look at all those hurts, feel the warmth of your own breath. Breathe kindness into your heart each time you breathe in. Feel the warmth filling up your heart.

Now think of the kindnesses you have performed for others, when you have given your time and energy to other beings—the times when you knew what was right and acted on that conviction. As you recall those moments, feel the hurts, and the belief that you don't belong, flow out of you with each exhalation.

Continue to breathe out those false beliefs. Allow them to be replaced by the knowledge that this body you inhabit, and the place it inhabits on this earth, are yours, and that you belong right where you are right now. Let the knowledge of your belonging, of your goodness, of your being enough, fill up your heart.

Emotional Geology

I swear the earth shall surely be complete to him or her
  who shall be complete,
The earth remains jagged and broken only to him or her
  who remains jagged and broken.

WALT WHITMAN, *THE SONG OF THE ROLLING EARTH*

In the midst of my depression, I tried to write about how
I felt. I wrote of a great dark pit—a chasm that terrified yet fasci-
nated me.

At first it was frightening and forbidding, the last place I
would want to explore, much less be near. But as I held that image,
I found after some time that I could go in and explore what there
was to see. No longer did I have the fear that I would fall in and
find that there was no bottom, only endless darkness. Instead, I
found that I could make excursions into this pit and that there was
much of interest to see.

The image changed. I could see plants and flowers and
trees that grew from the sides of the hole. Small animals lived in
there, drawing life from what little light there was. And rather than
bottomless darkness, I found a cool, sweet spring bubbling up from
the bottom.

There is a kind of spiritual mining that can be done in depression. The pit is just the beginning, like the entrance into the underworld spoken of in myth. There is much more to be found here
than a world of decay and death. The depths to be found in depression can be more like the underground world Alice found down
the rabbit hole—terrifying, yet strangely beautiful.

I no longer think of exploring depression as involving a

journey to the underworld. I envision depression instead as having a spiritual and emotional geology. Exploring that geology reveals gold, and gems.

In our digging and exploring, even those treasures are small stuff. We're after what is to be found much deeper. When we go down deep, past the surface of both our outer and inner worlds, past the incredibly rich soil where growth and decay cycle endlessly, we get to bedrock, to what is solid in our life.

Drill deeper, and beneath the rock is water. Here we find the cool springs, the underground lakes and rivers. These are what give us sustenance, provide the calm undercurrent. Here is the constant movement, the flowing and changing nature of our life, which lies beneath the seemingly solid foundation we imagine is there.

Down here, too, is the alchemical transformation of dead and rotten animals and plants. Changed through heat and pressure into fossil fuels, they become the light and energy of our life. They warm us, light our way, and help us along on our journey.

Finally, beneath all that is pure energy. Self-sustaining, not dependent on sunlight or wind or water, it is the molten core. Here we find the place where passion and desire are transformed, as rock is transformed into lava. Lava that flows finally to the surface, to again become rock, to create islands, continents, and new lands. It is the core that can transform our life as well. Here too we find the source of gravity, the force that emanates from the center to bind all things together, just as our life is intertwined with the life of all other beings.

Further Exploration

Earlier you may have pictured your depression as a place. You imagined a barren dessert, a thick forest, a misty ravine, or perhaps the bottom of the ocean. Now make a return visit there. Prepare the provisions and equipment you need. Then take a few excursions into this territory—short and slow trips at first.

Can you envision your depression in a different way? Rather than seeing it as an ugly, fearful, foreboding place, can you see it as a place to be explored, a place of possibility? Bring to your exploration a sense of curiosity, a sense of wonder. Is there beauty you may have missed the first time? Is there life you didn't see? Like an explorer in a new country, try not to see it through the lenses of your old world. What do you find there that interests you? That frightens you? That surprises or shocks you? Are there things you find that you can bring back out with you to help you in your daily journey? Can you come back with stories of wonder and adventure?

In such a journey, a person often does more than return with new experiences. The person is fundamentally changed. They have learned new lessons, or found a strength or wisdom they didn't know they had. When you take this journey into depression with an open mind and heart, what are the inner gifts you may come back with?

A Path through Depression

But what, O monks, is the noble truth of the path
leading to the extinction of suffering? It is the noble
eightfold path that leads to the extinction of suffering,
namely: perfect view, perfect thought, perfect speech,
perfect action, perfect livelihood, perfect effort, perfect
mindfulness, perfect concentration.

BUDDHA

The path is always right beneath your feet.

ISSAN DORSEY

When we are depressed, we can feel adrift in the world,
lost in our own lives. In the midst of this suffering we may welcome
any suggestions about how to find our way. If someone could only
lay out a clear, convincing path for us, we would follow it as quickly
and as carefully as we could.

But instead there seem no easy answers. Like Hansel and
Gretel, we find that the bread crumbs we left behind to show us the
way have been eaten, and we remain lost.

The difficulty in finding a path arises because human life
does not function in a programmatic way, even though often we
would like it to. There is no one answer, no series of steps that,
when followed, will solve our problems forever.

But we *can* find our way. Yet, rather than a way out, we can
find a way back into life. We can discover a path that is itself a way
of being in each moment.

When Buddha found a way through the suffering of life to
a place of peace and joy, he had both found and made a path. This

path, which he called the Eightfold Path, is available to anyone. It consists, not surprisingly, of eight elements: right view, right resolve, right speech, right conduct, right livelihood, right effort, right mindfulness, and right concentration.

The word *samma,* which describes each part of the path, is usually translated as "right," but the root meaning in Sanskrit is "complete" or "whole." These eight practices can lead to a more complete and full participation in our life. Each one expresses the fullness, healing, and harmony already present in our life.

The steps on this path are not sequential. Rather, they form a circle in which each step leads to, informs, and strengthens all the others.

The Eightfold Path does not lead to a goal. Instead, it is itself the embodiment of the goal. In setting foot on the path, we have already moved into the fullness of life.

The Eightfold Path can be divided into three areas: views or understanding, meditation, and ethical action. The practices of the Eightfold Path are not only readily available to us in our depression, but well suited to the particular suffering we are experiencing.

Depression affects our ability to think, creating dangerous and painful beliefs. By looking at those beliefs, and honestly seeing whether our experience upholds them, we can let go of many of them. When we come to a fuller understanding of ourselves and our lives, we can find an antidote to our suffering.

Depression also affects our ability to act. We may act in ways harmful to ourselves and others. Depression can also simply make it difficult for us to take *any* action. In either case, we can learn instead how to act in ways that are more harmonious and effective.

Finally, we often feel in depression that we are separated from our life. Depression strengthens many of the barriers that make a fuller experience of our lives difficult. When we meditate, we are engaging in what is at root a practice of being fully present in life, a way to be more intimate with all we encounter, from moment to moment.

Following the Eightfold Path may sound like a daunting task at first. Though it does require effort, it is not really a difficult journey. Indeed, it is not so much a path at all as it is a direction.

When we take this path, we choose to move toward joy, compassion, and service, and to turn from suffering and isolation. This turning takes place inside of us, so that once we have started, any direction we take becomes our path.

This path is a way of living. It is a way of acting, a way of dealing with ourselves and others. When we choose to follow this path, all that we encounter has the possibility of teaching us.

There are no wrong turns on this journey. Any way you choose provides an opportunity for practice and discovery.

Further Exploration

Return to the place you have imagined as your depression. If you have been here a number of times, you know this place well. You may even feel comfortable here. You have found it is no longer a terrifying place, and that there can be much of value in this place.

As you return, envision that in this place there is now a path to be found. Perhaps it is a trail that has been worn through the dark forest you were in, or a star to follow to guide yourself out of a deep desert night—or a lifeline you can follow from deep beneath the sea.

Look closely at this path, this trail, until it becomes clear to you. Realize that there is a way out of this place you once thought you would be lost in forever. Are you ready to leave? Are you perhaps surprised to find you are sad at the prospect of leaving? Are you ready to begin the journey? Is there freedom or relief in starting out on your way?

The Middle Way

The Middle Path opens the eyes, produces knowledge, and leads to peace, insight, and enlightenment.

BUDDHA

Two monks were arguing over a philosophical question as their teacher passed by. They stopped him and asked him to settle their disagreement. The first monk explained his understanding, to which their teacher replied, "You're right." The second monk protested, and made his argument, which was the complete opposite of what the first monk had said. The teacher then answered the second monk, saying, "You're right." A third monk who had been listening asked in frustration, "But, Master, you tell both of these monks that they are right, when their explanations are contradictory and couldn't possibly both be correct." The teacher replied, "You're right."

ZEN STORY

In depression all color seems to have drained out of the world. Everything seems black and white to us.

Depression increases our usual tendency to think in extremes of black and white. Nuances evade our grasp. Things either are or they aren't. Though it may take a while to come to a decision, when we do make a choice, it is usually an either/or decision. (In fact, part of our difficulty in making decisions stems from the fact that we are thinking in such stark terms, and have a hard time holding the subtleties of many possibilities in our minds.)

But though stark extremes may be comforting, they seldom describe the way things are. We need only look at ethnic, political, or religious wars to see where extreme views get us. While it is comforting to rest in extremes, as they can give us a comfortable certainty, this certainty is ultimately a painful illusion.

Buddha spoke of his teaching as being a middle path, between the extremes that he saw in his world at the time. These were the extremes of seeking peace in either sensual pleasures or ascetic practices. The middle path walks the line between selfishness and selflessness, between seeing existence as real and seeing it as an illusion.

This middle path is a difficult path to follow, because it is utterly dynamic. It often requires us to hold two contradictory ideas in our minds at the same time. It means balancing on the razor's edge, and avoiding the temptation of easy answers.

A short time ago I was at a funeral for a very kind man I had worked with. At the service the pastor asked for people in attendance to speak about their memories of Michael. Many people spoke of how kind and unselfish he was, how he often encouraged people, "You should have what you want."

For a moment no one spoke, and it seemed there might be nothing left to say. Then my friend Elaine, a grandmotherly woman, slowly rose to her feet. In the midst of all this reverence, her booming voice echoed. "On the other hand . . . ," she began, and proceeded to tell a story of how Michael had encouraged her to buy a coat she couldn't afford, telling her, "You should have what you want." She loved Michael, she said, but wanted him to know she was still paying for that coat.

In reminding us about the other side of things, Elaine wisely brought us all back into the middle, where the path to the truth is found.

To follow this path is to accept the tension between opposing views and possibilities. It is to know that both may be correct.

Practicing the middle way requires that we hold all beliefs and ideas loosely, and remain open to the possibility of change in what we believe or how we think.

In our struggle with depression, this can mean standing in the midst of uncertainty. The uncertainty between solving all our problems with medication, and refusing to consider medication as an option. The uncertainty between viewing depression as merely a physical illness, and viewing it as a condition brought on by psychological conditions and poor coping skills. The uncertainty between working hard to heal, and just letting go and giving up trying to force a solution.

The middle path requires that we look at all our actions and choices in the light of practicality. It also requires that we not lose sight of the spirituality that must undergird our decision. Ultimately we must avoid both fanaticism and indecisiveness, and look at what is called for in this moment.

Further Exploration

Identify a situation you have been having some difficulty with. It does not have to relate to your depression; it can be a job problem, a relationship trouble, a difficulty at home.

Now let the problem sit in your mind for a few minutes. Let it settle through the layers of your thoughts, floating downward of its own weight until it settles in your belly. As thoughts about what to do come up, simply note them.

Imagine the problem as hard and round and difficult to open. Let it be the object of your attention.

Now, as you examine the problem, let it split apart like the halves of an orange. Just look at it. Push these two halves as far apart as you can, as you polarize your two approaches to the situation. If you find yourself thinking about it in one way, push that view to an almost absurd extreme, and then consider what the opposite would be.

Continue to reflect on it in this way, until you have pushed these two halves as far apart as you believe you can. Imagine that you hold one in each hand, balancing their truth and reality in your hands. Can you see the truth in each of them?

Take that seed of truth in each one, and place both seeds in front of you. Let them sit there for a few minutes.

Can you find a way to proceed that avoids both these extremes and yet contains the seed of truth that is in each one? Continue to hold them separate as you move ahead along the path that threads its way in balance between them.

Notice your reaction or responses to difficult situations for a few days. Before responding to or acting on a situation, stop to consider its opposite as a valid way to respond. Can you use the opposite to temper your usual approach? Is there a middle path you can use to approach the problem?

Not What We Think

You cannot get it by taking thought;
You cannot seek it by not taking thought.

ZEN POEM

Often when we start out on the spiritual path, we think following it is just a matter of doing the right things. We hope that if we simply follow the rules or a certain code of behavior, we will find joy, or enlightenment, or peace.

This can especially be a problem for us in depression. We are often so desperate, in such pain, that we will follow anyone or anything that offers us easy answers and predetermined outcomes.

But the truth is that the spiritual path is never as simple as that. It's not what we think it is. At its heart it can never be simply a matter of following the right outward forms. In fact, truth is not to be found in thinking in any one particular way, or in acting in a certain manner. It's not to be found in wearing a particular kind of clothing, or in shaving your head, or in growing your hair long.

It's not about never feeling perturbed or bothered by suffering or disappointments in your life. It isn't found in wearing a mask of stillness at all times. It's not found in never thinking of yourself and in tirelessly doing things for others. And it's not found in thinking about yourself endlessly, either. In fact, it's not found in what you think at all.

Rather it is found in meeting everyone and everything with compassion and attentiveness. It is found in being present in our life with all our heart and all our mind. And, rather than in any set of beliefs or actions—anything we think we know—it is found in the willingness to *not* know, to keep the openness and curiosity we were born with.

Further Exploration

What are all the ways you have tried to find the truth, to find the peace and happiness you have sought? Most of them ended in disappointment. You discovered the hope and promise you thought you had found giving way to the feeling that you had turned down another dead end.

But there have been times when you felt that everything in the world was right, *when you felt truly at home in your life, a part of everything around you. You felt at peace, and you felt joy in your life, and you felt grateful to be alive.*

Perhaps it was a time when you were playing with your child, or just sitting with a close friend, or looking at the full moon. Or maybe you were doing nothing at all. Or perhaps you were even going through a painful or difficult time, but still things felt they were exactly as they should be right at that moment.

Think of one or two of those times. Look beyond the particular details of what was happening, to what you felt was beyond those details. Can you find what allowed you to see and feel this intimacy with yourself and your life? In that, you will begin to find the way.

The Final Authority

Be lamps unto yourselves.

BUDDHA

Of the two judges, trust the principal one.

TIBETAN PRACTICE SAYING

When we are in depression, we may find that the number of people who want to tell us what to do is limitless. We may become willing listeners because so many of us want to be told what to do. Indeed, when we feel most adrift, in doubt of our own judgment and unable to make any decision, all the people who have advice to offer can be very comforting. We want to have someone else show us the way.

Here is the secret. It is good news and bad news. The bad news is that no one else really knows what path is best for you, so they can't give you the answer. The good news is that since no one else really knows, the answers are to be found within you.

No one else can live your life for you, and no one else has to live with the consequences that will follow for you. Others are free to give you all kinds of solutions and advice, but it is all just so much opinion. They may tell you to see a counselor, or exercise harder, or take herbs, or change your diet, or take medication, or not take medication. But because no one else knows your total situation, don't be surprised if this advice leaves you more confused than before. And don't be surprised if the loudest and most vehement voices telling you what to do come from within.

To make your way through depression and find your way

through it to healing, you will need to listen to these many voices, and still make the choices on your own.

Your body and mind, your life, are different from anyone else's. As a Zen teacher has said, "You can't exchange even a single fart with anyone else." Your circumstances call for attentiveness and compassion, which must first come from you.

When, after some struggle, I came to realize that I was going through a depression, I found that all sorts of prejudices and preconceptions were present in my thinking. I had spent over a decade working with people dealing with mental illness, including a great number with depression. I could be understanding and accepting of *their* choices, and I encouraged them to keep an open mind about things such as counseling and medication. Unfortunately, I had no such understanding for myself. I felt that surely my own depression was the result of some weakness on my part, and that I did not need any outside help.

I had to look carefully at my preconceptions, and then start from what has been called "beginner's mind." Until I did this, I simply could not respond to my depression, and to my life, as I needed to in that moment.

As you follow the path of your own healing, remember that it is strictly your own path to follow. No one else can choose it for you, and no one else will follow it but you.

Many people come to a spiritual path looking for a person, a tradition, or a holy scripture that will tell them what to do, and how to act, and thus relieve them of the need to take any responsibility. What they finally learn, if they are fortunate, is that true spirituality requires not the relinquishing of responsibility, but the wholehearted acceptance of it.

Learn all you can about the illness, about the theories of its causes, about treatment options, and about what each option entails —and remember that the decision of how to proceed is yours and yours alone. You will know better than anyone else when something connects with your circumstances and values. In particular, you know best of all when something is helpful to you, when it will further your own healing, and when it will help you to function and live your life more fully.

As you do this, you will learn to trust yourself as the final authority. As you become more clearly and dispassionately aware of your feelings, thoughts, and sensations, and as you learn more about your depression, you will be able to better know when a treatment or action is helping. Whatever path you choose, you will also be better able to give information to the people you have chosen to help you, which will in turn allow them to more effectively help you.

Be ready for people to criticize whatever decisions you make. Even a casual look at the various theories and approaches to treating depression will show you that there are myriad approaches and ideas, many of them diametrically opposed to each other. Whatever you choose to do, someone will probably tell you that it is wrong. In those moments, remind yourself that the truth often lies between the extremes of competing ideas.

Don't hold too tightly to any idea or approach, even after you have started with it. But don't discard it too quickly, either. Be patient and give it some time to work. At the same time, if it does become obvious that it is not working, let it go. Allow your ideas and preconceptions about treatment, therapy, or medication to turn out to be wrong.

You remain the one final authority for your life. But as the bumper sticker says, question authority—even your own. Be flexible, be confident, and be kind to yourself as you make mistakes and follow your path.

If you can learn to do this in the midst of depression, you will be able to do it at just about any time in your life, whatever situation you find yourself in.

Further Exploration

In becoming able to look at yourself as the final authority, it is helpful to first identify whom you see now as your authorities. When you don't know what to do, whom do you turn to? What does the desperation feel like when you don't know what to do? Do you feel you must have someone else decide for you?

Once you have identified your authorities, can you decide that you will listen to their opinions, but not take what they say as the final word?

Sit quietly, watching your breath.

Look past the mind that worries about who is right and what others will think of you. Go within to find that place where a wise being sits with you when you sit. Acknowledge this being. Imagine this being in whatever way you choose, whether in traditional representation or a more modern manner.

Now look at the being's face. See that the calm face is none other than your own. Breathe in as you feel that you are eye-to-eye with the wise being. Ask a question if you wish. Or just sit in silence, breathing together. With an inner bow that is an act of recognition rather than of worship, leave the being's presence, and return to watching your own breath. Remember that this wisdom waits always for you, whenever you need it.

Community

It may seem that I have locked myself away
from the people of the world, and yet, why is it
I have never ceased to think of them?

RYOKAN

The Sanskrit word *sangha* refers to the community of people who practice Buddhism. It originally meant the community of monks, but through the years its meaning expanded to include the lay community as well. Some teachers have expanded the term further, until it essentially includes all sentient beings. This is not that far off, since, as Buddha said, "I was enlightened together with all beings."

In Buddhism *sangha* is considered a jewel or treasure precisely because it can be an aid to us as we travel the spiritual path. Of course, like any community, it can also be a source of frustration, and at times it may even seem a hindrance.

Sangha has been likened to a tumbler full of stones. As all the stones roll around and bump up against each other, their rough edges are worn off, and they begin to become smooth. When we finally take them out, they look nothing like they did before they went in. Not only are they smooth, but they reveal new beauty, with colors and patterns that couldn't be seen before.

When we are in depression, we may feel cut off from any kind of community. The thick curtain that seems to envelop us keeps us isolated and makes it hard for us to reach out to others. It is especially difficult to connect when others offer us advice, or tell us what to do.

We may try to talk to friends about what is happening to us, but most people can listen for only so long to our thoughts and fears—and to our talk of desperation, hopelessness, and pain—before they feel compelled to stop us or turn away. It is difficult for others to listen, because our words touch some fears and grief within them in their own lives.

Even for those who do want to hear, who listen and try to be truly present for us, it is as if we are sending dispatches from a far-off country. We tell them about the sights and sounds of a land they have not seen, and our words limit us in what we can communicate to them. Our fears are difficult to put into words. Though we need human connection now more than ever, we may end up feeling frustrated and thwarted in our attempts to speak to others.

The example of self-help groups—which rediscovered the value of *sangha* in this century—can help us here. It can be immensely healing to speak to another person who knows or has experienced what we are going through. We can learn that we are not alone, and that others have been through depression and survived. They may even have experiences and insights that can help us. When we are with these people, we don't need to expend a lot of energy trying to explain what we are going through. It is a huge relief to at last be understood.

It is possible to find someone—or perhaps several people—for whom just a few words tell everything we need them to know. We can then feel heard, and acknowledged, and understood. Often with such a person we don't even have to speak at all. We know there are no expectations for us when we are with that person.

A person who has been through their own depression can be more courageous with us. They know depression, and so they fear it less than others who haven't been there. They are living proof that you can survive. They can tell you what helped them and let you know how it may work for you. Their words carry the authority of experience.

Many people in the helping professions, and many spiritual teachers and counselors, have not been through what you are experiencing. They may be knowledgeable in their areas of expertise, but they may lack the understanding, the common ground, the visceral experience, to truly connect with someone in the depths of depression.

Intimate communication with someone who has explored the same interior landscape can bring us safety and hope. Through these, we may find the strength to move once again into our larger community. We can begin to heal and move through the barrier of depression to a place where we can be a part of the community of all beings again.

A wise friend, who shared with me his own struggle with depression, put it well. "It's as though," he said, "we are both at different points midway up a steep, dangerous cliff. We aren't sure whether we can go up or down. And we must give nearly all of our energy to the dangerous situation we both find ourselves in, so we can offer each other very little real help. But what a relief just to have someone else on this cliff to talk with, someone to ask, 'What's the path look like for you? Are you scared? Does it look like a long way down?'"

To have a companion on any path is no small gift.

Further Exploration

Sit quietly with a loved one, watching your breathing together. You may both face forward. Or if you feel enough trust, and are able to, you may sit facing each other and look into each other's eyes.

Sit in silence, watching your own breath, sharing the moment. Take comfort and pleasure in sensing the other person's presence, hearing their gentle breathing at the same time they are listening to yours.

If they shift on their pillow, acknowledge that they are facing the same restlessness and perhaps discomfort that you are.

Continue sitting, resting in the knowledge that you don't have to go through your life always alone, but knowing that there are others who can be with you on your journey, even as they make their own way.

When you have finished, bow to each other, or in some other way acknowledge what you have just shared.

After sitting with your friend, or at another time, take a walk or eat a meal together in silence and mindfulness. Again, just share in the pleasure and comfort of doing this in another's presence.

At any one time, one out of seven women, and one out of twelve men, are dealing with depression. Take the risk of reaching out to someone else you know who is also going through depression. Let them know that you are dealing with the same thing, and ask if they would like to get together so the two of you can share your struggles. You may even want to set up regular meetings for this. Let them know that since you know what depression is like, you won't feel hurt if they don't return a call right away, or just aren't up to meeting with you.

Faith

There is nothing that persuades us or pushes us or forces
us to create faith. Faith means tranquillity, and complete
tranquillity is the source of our nature and our existence.

DAININ KATAGIRI ROSHI

It's hard to have faith in anything when the present moment is so painful. If faith were based only on hope, it would have
no foundation when all hope is gone. But when we are beyond
hope, what are we left with?

We are left with ourselves—our own mind and body. And
we can take faith that within our life, and within our own experience, we can find the answers we are looking for.

In Buddhism, faith is to be found in the understanding that
Buddha did find solutions to the problem of suffering in our lives.
But even this starting point is not taken blindly; rather, it is something that is confirmed by our experience. And as we go forward,
we continue to seek an understanding that is confirmed first and
foremost by our own experience.

In our depression we can have faith in the answers that
others before us have found. We can see that others have recovered
from depression and take faith that we can do the same. And within
our own experience, our own body and mind, we can find the answers we need to heal from our depression.

Oddly enough, we can also take faith in one of the very
things that bring some of our pain. We can trust in impermanence,
which in depression we see all too clearly. Rather than being a matter for further hopelessness, impermanence can offer us some hope.

Only the fact that all things are impermanent makes any change possible. Things may in this moment be difficult, but we can be certain that they will change. Though we are not certain what form the next moment will take, in that very uncertainty lies our opportunity.

In depression it seems that we have always been depressed and will always be depressed. But here impermanence helps us as well. Most depressions end after some time, even if we do nothing about them.

Though in depression we can feel stuck, as though we were standing still in the midst of a rapidly spinning world, we are part of the changing world as well. So we can have faith in the possibility of change and the possibility of an end to our suffering. This faith is based ultimately on faith in ourselves.

At times we may feel beyond hope. But hope implies doing nothing, taking no active part, and waiting for a healing change to occur. Instead, we can have faith—faith that leads us to effort. This faith and this effort can bring us closer to what we seek—and in the process, both faith and effort can grow and strengthen.

Selflessness

"Who are *you*?" said the Caterpillar.

Alice replied, rather shyly, "I—I hardly know, Sir, just at present—at least I know who I *was* when I got up this morning, but I must have changed several times since then."

LEWIS CARROLL, *ALICE'S ADVENTURES IN WONDERLAND*

To study the Buddha way is to study the self. To study the self is to forget the self. To forget the self is to be enlightened by all things.

DOGEN, *GENJOKOAN*

In depression it may seen that our very self is disintegrating. Nothing we do seems to make any difference. We don't know who we are or where we fit in. This can be confusing at best, and terrifying at worst.

Buddhism has extensively investigated this notion of a self and concluded that, in fact, there is no such thing as a separate, concrete, unchanging self. (Buddhism calls this lack of a permanent self one of the "marks of existence," along with suffering and impermanence.) Even for a longtime student of meditation, this can be a troubling concept, one that is difficult to understand and accept. And as an actual experience, it can be terrifying at first.

Our initial response to this notion of no separate self is often disbelief. Our experience tells us that there is an independent, concrete self. Any other view seems far-fetched or absurd. But if we look into it further, we can begin to understand what this idea is about. We may even begin to make some sense of what we are experiencing in our depression.

Our habitual belief in a separate, differentiated self is very important to us. Indeed, it is an essential part of our development as children. We all remember the intense need in adolescence to show that we are different, that we are individual, and that we matter.

As adults as well, we have all had the experience of consciously creating an apparent self, perhaps for a job interview, or for a high school reunion, or when we've fallen in love. We created a self—a set of images and actions—and then put it forth in the world and defended it.

Yet Buddhism tells us that this self is only an artificial creation.

What we normally think of as an unchanging, separate self is in fact a dynamic process, a process that is constantly in flux. Science tells us that all the cells in our bodies change completely every seven years. And our thoughts and perceptions change far faster still.

Interdependence is at the root of our existence. We are entangled with all other things in this world. We exist because of a myriad of causes and forces, and we live among a myriad of other beings, within the web of all life. So rather than imagining a self that somehow exists within this body and forms the center of the world, we can more accurately say that our self in fact *is* the whole world.

What does this have to do with depression? In depression there is an opening in the chatter of our minds, and of memory constantly creating a history. In this space we can begin to see the truth of this lack of a separate, abiding self. We may also find this truth through meditation, or during a tragedy, or in any activity where we "lose ourselves." It is exhilarating and liberating—and, sometimes, disorienting and frightening at the same time.

In one sense, depression is an illness in which the illusory self seems to disintegrate. At the same time, however, the self seems to be more substantial, because the suffering this ostensible self experiences is so intense. This makes depression particularly fertile ground for examining and investigating just what it is we refer to when we say "I" or "me."

If we can soften to our pain and not harden ourselves against it, we can begin to move into a sense of ourselves as softer and less substantial as well. We can experience ourselves as more spacious and open, as encompassing the whole world.

Depression, which in some ways can deaden our awareness and isolate us, can also point us to an important truth. Within that truth we can see that we are not isolated from the world. Indeed, we can see that we are none other than the world itself.

Further Exploration

Sitting and watching your breath, focus on your thoughts. Do they remain constant? Are you "thinking" them? Do they sometimes arise on their own? Are memories a great part of your thoughts? Is planning for the future? Does this give continuity to the arising and falling of thoughts? Do you find your self in your thinking?

Observe your sensations. Is there anything constant there? Is your self to be found in your sensations? In your body? Or when you think of your self, is there something more that it means to you?

Observe your feelings. As they come and go, do you see patterns or habits in your reactions? Is your self found in your feelings, or in those patterns? Is this who you are?

Look at the one who watches those thoughts, feelings, and sensations. Is this where your self lies? Where does this watcher go when you are not paying attention?

Do you find all these things—thoughts, feelings, and sensations—constantly changing? Sometimes thoughts predominate, sometimes feelings, sometimes sensations. Is this process you?

If you sit quietly, just watching your breath, is there a moment when this process is calm and quiet? Is there a moment when there are *no thoughts, no feelings, no sensations—just breathing in and out? Where are you then?*

Throughout the day, stop to observe yourself. What do you identify as your self? Is it your feelings? Your thoughts? Your sensations? Your body? Is there consciousness that is you?

Is there something constant that gives a thread of continuity, something that could be this self?

Do you fulfill several roles throughout the day—parent, lover, friend, worker, boss, teacher? Which of these is you? You interact with your world and other people throughout the day. Are you this activity? If so, where do you go when you are still and silent?

If your thoughts, feelings, and sensations are not you, if your roles are not you, if your body is not you—can you find this self anywhere?

Embedded in Life

To be enlightened by all things is to remove
the barriers between one's self and others.

DOGEN, *GENJOKOAN*

When we are depressed, our feelings of being separate from
our life and from others may seem overwhelming. We feel like we
live behind a curtain. At times this curtain may seem to be made of
thick black velvet—at other times of iron. At still other times it may
let some light through. But it is always there, making it difficult or
impossible to see and touch our lives, and for us to be seen and
touched.

Buddha spoke about this feeling of separateness. It is partly
the result of creating a separate self, and then protecting that self
from others at all costs. Yet we don't realize that what we really are
protecting is only the *illusion* of that separate self.

In contrast to the notion that we are each a separate self
that is independent and doesn't need anyone else, Buddha taught
that all things are interconnected and interdependent. A contempo-
rary Zen teacher, Thich Nhat Hanh, speaks of this connectedness as
"interbeing." As he explains it, innumerable things are present in
this very page, all of which need to be present for this piece of
paper to exist. The sunlight, rain, earth, and air that grew the trees
were necessary. The people who cut down the trees, processed the
paper, made the book, and brought it to you are also all involved
with this piece of paper. Include all the people and things that were
needed for *those* people's lives to come into being, and you can
begin to see how this piece of paper connects with the whole universe.

A Zen grace said before meals puts it this way: "Innumerable labors have brought us this food. We should be aware of how it comes to us." Not thankful for how it comes to us, but first of all aware. In that knowledge, thankfulness naturally follows.

In depression we forget how we are all interconnected. Our feelings of separateness are magnified. If you have felt that you never really fit in (and most of us have, at least in some ways or at some times in our lives), then this feeling may reappear or become greatly magnified. It can be very helpful to keep reminding ourselves that this feeling of separateness is in fact a case of mistaken identity.

We are seeking a true relationship and intimacy with all things. Yet this relationship does not need to be sought, since it is always and already there. It is in fact available to us in any moment we choose.

It is available to us because there is nothing to life *but* relationship; we are *already* in relationship with all things in every moment.

In times when you feel irredeemably separate, remember that you live embedded in the very midst of life. You cannot be separated from life any more easily than the flecks of obsidian can be separated from a piece of granite, or the molecules of oxygen can be removed from the air around you.

Further Exploration

Sitting quietly, bring your attention to your breath. Settling into your seat, feel how you are grounded and anchored to the earth, how it supports you and your life. Bring your awareness to this place where you sit as the center of an endless web, connecting all beings in this world to each other and to you.

In this web all beings are valued and important, all are necessary. These beings support your life at the same time as they need your existence to live.

As you breathe out, remember that your breath provides nourishing air to trees and plants, and in their breathing out lies your next breath.

In the immensity of this world each being is a part of all others, and contains all others. You are a part of this world; you breathe with all other beings. You are not separate from this world. You feel disconnected only because you have forgotten your membership in this family, which you can never be separated from.

This world supports you and your life as the very air supports everyone and everything.

With each breath, remember you are connected to the vast world. You have been embedded in this world from the moment you were born, and will remain linked with all beings until you take your last breath.

No Expectations

That doesn't mean we shouldn't set things up for
the future. It does mean that we would do well not
to become attached to particular outcomes. We'd
do better focusing our effort on being present rather
than on insisting on what the future must be.

STEVE HAGEN

Expect nothing.

PETER MATTHIESSEN

In depression we may spend most of our time with great
expectations. We grasp for something, anything, that promises an
end to our suffering, and place all of our hopes on that. Or else we
give in to the bleak future that the depression would have us believe
in, and give up all hope.

Yet, choosing *either* alternative is still living in our expectations. When we expect relief—or more suffering—we forget where
we are right now, and we give up on this moment. Yet it is only in
this moment, and nowhere else, that human beings can experience
joy, connection, and healing.

Expectations keep us out of this present moment. We may
expect that because of therapy, dietary changes, or medication, our
depression will end. We hope for positive results—maybe even enlightenment—from our meditation. Yet all of this is about the future. When we are caught up in the future, we are no longer present
with what we are doing right now, but looking ahead to the results.

Meditation is one thing we can do with no regard for what
it will bring us. We do it just to do it. If we use meditation or some

other spiritual practice to obtain something, to improve or advance ourselves in some way, then we are using it as we use everything else in our lives. It is just like the expensive car, the right clothes, the right relationship, and all those things that we hope will bring us happiness in some future moment.

Instead, we can remember that this moment, as it is, has everything we need within it. We have everything we need within us in this moment, also. We just need to be here and take care of our lives in this moment.

A popular affirmation has it that "every day in every way I'm getting better and better." What this implies, however, is that you're not good enough right in this moment. In meditation, we can begin to see that things are already perfect as they are. In such a world, we do not need self-help. Instead we can practice no-self, no-help.

To have no expectations also is to have an open mind, a beginner's mind. It is to hold to the profoundly valuable doubt of curiosity and questioning. It is to let go of our hopes of controlling an outcome. It is to give our heartfelt, compassionate attention to ourselves and all beings we meet in this moment, and to leave the future to the future.

To have no expectations is to commit ourselves fully to human life.

When we have no expectations, we give ourselves over to mystery. We ready ourselves for the wonder that may wait for us in any moment.

Further Exploration

As you sit quietly, pay attention to how you expect and anticipate the end of a period of sitting quietly. Perhaps you are using an alarm clock, or perhaps you are sitting with someone else, who will ring a bell when you are done.

Do you focus on being done? Do your expectations that now the clock will ring, now the time has to be up, grow until you are not paying attention to anything happening right now?

Can you put all this aside and just focus on each moment as it comes?

Before you begin sitting quietly, examine your expectations for how the next few minutes will go. Do you feel calm, so you are sure you will be able to remain still and quiet? Or perhaps your back hurts, and you are sure you will have a difficult time.

Do these expectations come to pass? How do your expectations color what does happen?

Can you acknowledge your expectations and then let things happen as they will, without regard to what you expect? How does it feel to sit with such an openness?

Close to the Truth

The truth shall set you free.

JESUS

I went once to speak with my Zen teacher, Katagiri Roshi, about an obstacle in the way of my meditation. I told him I had no difficulty with committing to the Buddhist teaching, or to him as a teacher. But, I said, I was having trouble committing to the idea of *sangha*—the local Zen Buddhist community—as the Buddhist tradition urges us to do.

Katagiri listened to all I had to say. Then he replied, "Why are you so worried about this? Why don't you just take a vow to commit to the truth, wherever you find it?"

I felt relieved, as though I had just been given complete permission to be myself. Only later did I begin to realize what a difficult charge I had been given.

Katagiri knew I was also studying aikido at the time. In a few phrases he expressed the main ideas of that practice, though he seemingly knew little about it. He asked, "In aikido, don't you try to stay close to your opponent, since to stay close to them is really the safest place to be? It is much the same with searching for the truth." He rolled his hands over and over each other and said, "When you are close to the truth, that too is the safest place to be. The truth can't hurt you when you are there."

Years earlier I had had an intense experience during a meditation retreat, where I had come close to some truths. But the experience of truth scared me, and I spent much of my time for a while afterward trying to get as far away from it as I could. Unfortunately, the frightening—and wonderful—thing about seeing the truth is that you can't forget it once you have seen it, and you can't get away from it, either. You may try to outrun it, but the truth will haunt you until you accept it—and, more important, act on it, if that is what it asks of you.

In our depression we sometimes come face-to-face with bare and frightening truths. And it can be tempting, given our state, to try to run away from them. Yet we can remember that to do so will only cause us more pain and suffering down the road.

So be gentle on yourself if you do take steps back from the truth—but remember that the safest place to be is close to it.

Further Exploration

There are probably a number of truths in your life that you have been afraid to acknowledge. Starting from a place of simple curiosity, think of one of those truths. Perhaps you hate your job and want to quit; perhaps there is something you have always dreamed of doing that you've never tried and never told anyone else about; perhaps you aren't as close to your child, friend, or partner as you would like to be.

As you think of this truth, notice—and set aside—your thoughts of self-blame and criticism for not having faced it before. (Notice how these thoughts may distract you from actually examining the situation.) Look at your fear at acknowledging this truth. Do you worry that you will have to act on it? Does it cause you pain to accept this truth? You don't need to think about what this truth requires of you. It needs only to be seen and acknowledged.

Allow this truth to stand before you. Let it be just what it is, without any fears or criticisms or anger.

Look directly at the situation contained in this truth. Do not push it away, and at the same time do not run from it, but simply stand your ground and meet it calmly. Stay with it and simply become friendly with it, getting to know it rather than determining what needs to be done in regard to it.

Realize now that you have let it into your circle of awareness—and that you can return to this truth and face it again whenever you choose.

Gratitude

> A man went to see a woman who was renowned for
> her wisdom, and asked her for advice. She told him,
> "Whatever happens to me, I always say, 'Thank you for
> everything. I have no complaints.'" The man went away
> but returned sometime later. "I have tried your advice,
> but do not feel any different," he told her. She replied,
> "Thank you for everything. I have no complaints."
> At this the man was enlightened.
>
> ZEN STORY

> If the only prayer you say in your whole life is "Thank you,"
> that would suffice.
>
> MEISTER ECKHART

When we are depressed, we are hard-pressed to find anything to be grateful for. We feel only pain and hopelessness. Even
the gift of being alive seems more a curse than a blessing.

How can we truly cultivate gratitude in our hearts? Is it the
words or thoughts, or is it a state of mind?

We may try to feel gratitude, but it can feel instead like it
did when we were children—a mere formality. (I remember so many
meals as a child when I would say grace just to be done with it, so
that I could simply plow into the food.) And when we go about life
mindlessly, not only do we have no appreciation for all we are
given; we are in fact disrespectful to all these gifts.

With the slowing down we experience in depression, we
are given the opportunity to experience and express a deeper gratitude. Large tasks can be overwhelming for us, but we can focus and

be attentive to the small things. Rather than racing through our life, as we may do when we are not depressed, in depression we can take the time to be present in each small action we perform. Perhaps we are unable to cook a seven-course meal, but we can still savor the can of beans or the sandwich we have put together. We can eat slowly and taste each bite of whatever food we have.

We are accustomed to thinking of gratitude only in terms of receiving. In doing so, we overlook what we already have. The difficulty we have in depression in being thankful for what we are given can lead us to gratitude for the most basic things, those things we already have. We are depressed, and we are suffering, but we can still be aware of all the small wonders that make up our human world— tasting, breathing, walking, being alive.

We can aim at such a mind of gratitude in any moment, simply by fully experiencing whatever is given to us. We can use up each moment of our life fully. When we live in this way, we take each moment as an offering, while at the same time making an offering of ourselves to each moment.

Further Exploration

Find a quiet space. Think of all that you are grateful for. This wondrous body that you inhabit, with its ability to see, hear, taste, touch, think, and feel.

Be aware of all the beings who support your life. Your family, your friends, your parents who gave you this life. All those people who grow your food, who work to make the clothes you wear, the house you live in. As you think of them, bring each one into your heart. Thank them, and give a nod of appreciation to them and their lives.

Think of the earth and its beings, with all that they provide. The ground you walk on, the plants or animals who sustain your life, the trees that clean the air you breathe. The sun that warms this earth. The clouds that rain down water. The stars that shine their beauty at night. Thank all of them.

Say grace before your meal. This can be a thanks to God, to the earth, or to the food. Or simply a moment of silence before diving into eating. Whatever feels best to you.

Just pause to give this thanks, this attention to the moment, before eating. Then eat slowly, maintaining this sense of gratitude throughout the meal. Savor the tastes, in the awareness that to do so is to give thanks continually.

How does it feel to say or perform this grace? Is it awkward? Or comforting? Is it easier to eat slowly and mindfully when you pause for grace first?

Attention

Zuigan Gen Osho called to himself every day, "Master!"
and answered, "Yes, sir!" Then he would say, "Be wide
awake!" and answer, "Yes, sir!"

MUMONKAN, CASE 12

It is amazing, when we stop to notice, how seldom we pay
attention throughout our day. We get ready in the morning and drive
to work in a fog. Sometimes during the day we may suddenly stop,
as though waking from sleep, and see how we have been mindlessly
going about our activities.

Our reactions—particularly to pain—are nearly always automatic. Many times we might just as well be asleep, considering
how little we really live and pay attention to our life.

Depression seems to put us even more to sleep. It dulls our
minds, making it more difficult for us to pay attention. At the same
time, we can become so tangled up in the pain of depression that
we aren't aware of it. All of our energy goes to fighting the pain.
And this fight makes our waking sleep even deeper.

Yet no matter how asleep we may be, it is possible to awaken.
Each of us can wake up, and continue to awaken, through the simple process of cultivating attention.

Attention enables us to step back from our waking dream,
while at the same time bringing us closer to a true encounter with
our life. It serves to clear out all that we add to this bare moment,
and lets us see it as it is.

Meditation is practice in attending. As we learn to pay attention to our mind and body, we see all the ways we forget to be
aware, and we pull ourselves back, over and over, to the experience
of this moment. In so doing we gradually become better at staying

present—at first in our meditations, and later in the rest of our life as well.

In depression we may feel like we are sleepwalking through life. Often this is how other people describe us. One of the best antidotes to this mindlessness is simply to be aware of it, to pay direct attention to it. In this way we can choose not to let depression steal our experience of life from us.

The word *attention* means "the act of attending." At its best, this can mean attending to our life, and the life of the world around us, as we might attend to a small child—being truly caring and present with the child. At the very least, when we feel we are passing through our life without really experiencing it, we can take a step toward full, compassionate participation by beginning with the other sense of *attending*. We can begin simply by showing up for our life.

Further Exploration

Shikantaza, *the Zen meditation practice of choiceless awareness, is said to allow the mind to take its natural form—open, unperturbed, and spacious as the great blue sky.*

Sitting quietly, begin to focus and calm yourself by watching and following your breath. When you feel sufficiently settled, try to practice this choiceless awareness.

Take no particular object as the focus of your meditation; rather, nurture a state of open awareness, so that whatever occurs inside or outside of you is allowed to pass through the open sky of your awareness like clouds. Let it all come and go through your body and mind. Notice sensations, thoughts, breathing, emotions, and sounds, but do not focus on any of them.

Remain in this state of open awareness. Reside in that quietness and attentiveness of one who listens for something small but important.

Allow yourself to fill with and be emptied of all that is happening within and without you, letting sights and sounds and smells pass through you as they would through a screen door in the summer.

Sit Down

Why don't you just sit down and shut up?

DAININ KATAGIRI ROSHI

In depression it seems that there is a barrier between ourselves and our lives. Meditation is concerned with breaking through that barrier, and so it can be a very appropriate practice for us. Meditation is one of the few things that can be done well in the midst of depression, because all it requires of us is that we sit down, be quiet, and pay attention.

When we feel that we can't do anything right, and that doing anything at all requires extreme effort, meditation is a wonderful practice, because it is at once rigorous and gentle. The vast open sky that is meditation is large enough to hold our depression. We don't have to feel that we must leave our depression out; it can be brought along with us into our meditation.

In the sitting meditation taught by Dogen there is no thought of gain or loss, of progress to be made, or of enlightenment to be found. It is done simply to explore the moment as fully as possible.

We make full effort—but this is meditation, not Marine boot camp. Pain comes up, and we make our best effort not to be overcome by it or let it cause us to give up. On the other hand, we do not seek pain in our sitting practice, and if it is too great we can take a break.

You don't need to sit in meditation for any certain length of time—only as long as you are able. There is no wrong way to do it. If you can maintain your attention on your breath for only one or two seconds, that is what you do. To scold or judge yourself is not part of meditation. (It may be a part of your depression, but meditation can help to soften that judgmental voice.)

You need only stop, sit down, breathe, and pay attention with all your heart. Don't compare this moment with your meditation yesterday, or last week, or two minutes ago. Right now, just do the best you can.

Meditation is nothing special or exotic. Instead, it is simply slowing down to listen to what is within us and around us. It is paying attention with our heart and our mind to each moment as it presents itself to us.

Meditation is done with our mind and heart, but it is also done with our body. Pay attention to how your body is sitting. Keep your spine straight, rather than letting it bend or sway. And if the pain of sitting becomes overwhelming, either change your position or stop.

When I went to see my Zen teacher for the first time after I had started meditating, I had all kinds of questions about philosophy, about all the fantastic things I had read. But Katagiri Roshi wouldn't hear much of it that day. He wanted to know how my breathing was going, if my posture was solid and balanced. I mentioned the pain in my legs, and he suggested I work toward sitting meditation in the half-lotus position, even if only for a short time. He suggested I start by sitting that way in the tub.

That was it. No lofty philosophical discussions, just questions about my knees and my breathing.

The ideal way to practice meditation is to do it each day. Something happens with regular meditation practice, with the commitment to meditate on both good days and bad days.

First of all, daily practice lets us begin to see that in fact there is no such thing as good or bad meditation. We simply make our best effort. Some days our mind is quiet, our body feels comfortable, and we find a period of cooling silence and joy. Other days it is not so easy. But we still sit down and see what there is within us and around us in *this* moment.

We can deal with our depression in much the same way. Each day, good or bad, we make our best effort. We pay attention to how we are feeling. We meet our depression and see it as it is, in this and each moment.

Further Exploration

Sitting comfortably and feeling your breathing in your belly, practice settling in to your meditation.

Imagine that you are a pebble settling in a swiftly flowing stream, falling down through the current until you have settled with your full weight on the sandy bottom. Feel the weight of your body as it presses down on your seat and the back of your legs and your knees. Concentrate on your breath as it settles down into your body and tethers you to the ground on which you sit.

If you feel an urge to stand up, or feel energy lifting you up, think of this as just the current, temporarily lifting you off the bottom of the stream. Then quickly settle back onto the bottom.

As you fill with your breath, notice how the energy of it pulls you down and you settle where you are. As your outbreath empties you, feel how you grow heavier and settle again.

Keep your awareness in your belly and on your seat. If your thoughts pull you up, simply think, "Settling," and return to your belly and your seat. Notice how your intention to keep settled anchors you to the bottom.

Practice walking very slowly with awareness, concentrating on the thought and feeling of settling. As you breathe in and raise your foot, feel again the downward energy that pulls you back to the earth. As you exhale and set your foot back down, feel your full weight on that foot.

Move as a pebble is pushed along the bottom of a stream, too heavy to be lifted up, but just pushed along the bottom. Notice when you forget to pay attention to this settling. If your thoughts lighten and pull you up, feel again the energy of the downward motion in your walking, and gently return to settling.

Throughout the day, at least once every few hours, think, "Settle." Notice when it is that you seem to rise up out of yourself. Let yourself settle into your life and who you are, and notice how the breath flows down into your belly, tethering and settling you.

Four Horses

A fine horse runs at even the shadow of a whip.

BUDDHA

Buddha told a story about the four types of horses and the ways they learn and respond to their master.

The first horse responds to the shadow of the whip; the second to the sound of the whip; and the third to the feeling of the whip on its skin. But the fourth horse does not respond until it feels the pain of the whip in its bones and marrow.

Buddha drew a comparison between these horses and the way we as spiritual seekers respond to the guidance we receive and the pain we experience in our lives.

Most of us would like to be the first type of horse, or at least the second or third. If asked, we would like to say that we can learn and respond quickly. We don't want to learn things the hard way. We don't want to have to wait until we are down on our knees before we make a change.

But the fact is that most of us are like the fourth horse. We don't change until the pain is so great that we can't take it any longer.

We may secretly know this but feel there is something wrong or shameful about it—that to be like the fourth horse is to be slow or stupid. And this is the last thing we want to admit when we are in the midst of depression.

But this story can give us some perspective. It can help us have some understanding and acceptance of ourselves.

We *don't* have to think we are stupid or slow. Instead, we can simply say to ourselves, "Ah, I am like the fourth horse, because I am human."

In fact, there is real value in being like the fourth horse. Because we need to feel the pain in our bones and marrow, we can be sure that when we do learn a lesson, we have learned it not just on a surface level, but deeply: we have taken it into ourselves. When the time comes for us to remember that lesson and use it in our life, we can do so all the more effectively because we have learned it so deeply.

We can also look at the story of the four horses as a description of the process of learning. We can learn *not* to have to feel the whip in our bones and marrow every time, but to respond at the feel of the whip on our skin and muscle the next time around.

In depression we may feel pain and suffering in our bones and marrow, and we may at last begin to respond to this pain. We may also feel we are slow and stupid because it took so long for us to begin to look at the causes of our pain.

It does not really matter whether this is so. What matters is that we are here, and we are learning from our pain now. You would not even be reading this book if you were not ready to do something about your pain. This demonstrates that you can learn and you can heal.

Actually, there is also a fifth horse, one that does not run regardless of the strength of the whip or the pain it causes. Your speed in changing and healing is not important. So long as you are responding and learning—that is the important thing.

Homelessness

Cold Mountain is a house without beams or walls. The
six doors left and right are open, the hall is blue sky.

HAN SHAN

A home is a safe place to go—asylum in the truest sense of
the word. James Hillman has said that home and family are where
we can feel comfortable and safe in regressing.

But depression can make us feel as if we are adrift, homeless in this world. We may feel this so acutely that we cope by literally staying inside of our own home and never going out.

As the old blues song has it, home is in our head. Yet in depression, when we try to find that feeling of centeredness and safety
within ourselves, we can't find it anywhere. So we hide inside our
room with curtains drawn, and we try to lock the perils of the outside world away behind the door.

When we can't find our home, we can look for help to
those who choose to have no home. In the days since Buddha, monks
have left their homes, families, and possessions to follow and practice Buddhism. ("Home leaver" is a term for a Buddhist monk.) In
the beginning there were no huge monasteries. The monks lived in
the forest, existing on what they received during their daily rounds
of begging. What can we learn from these people?

This: in one sense we are all homeless. What we call home
is fragile and temporary. Even this planet is a place where we stay
for only a short time.

People who wish to follow in Buddha's footsteps tradition-
ally take three vows, which involve "taking refuge" in Buddha (the
teacher), the truth (*dharma* in Sanskrit), and the Buddhist community

(sangha). My teacher, Katagiri Roshi, told us that when we take these vows we become refugees. He was not just making a clever turn of phrase. When we throw ourselves into the spiritual life ("Buddha's world," as he put it), we do so without guarantee, without expectation, without any promise of reward or of finding something lasting. We place ourselves fully into the world of impermanence. Once we have done so, it is hard to return to old ways of thinking and living.

Buddhism changed through the centuries. The monks began growing their own food and eventually built great monasteries to live in. Yet this idea of becoming homeless continues to define the life of a monk. It has continued because there is a valuable lesson in the teaching.

Depression gives us a chance to taste and touch more clearly the sense of leaving home, of having no home. Once we have touched it, we return again to the question of how we live.

Yet meditation may be a kind of home. It is a place we can return to again and again, where we can settle in with all of our fears and sadness and grief. It can teach us to live in the truth that we do not really have a home.

In meditation we have taken the ultimate step, sitting there naked in the world. In that place, the whole world ultimately becomes our home.

Further Exploration

Sitting quietly, begin watching your breath. Feel the weight of your body on your seat. Feel the confines of this body that is your home. Let yourself settle fully into your body, and think, "Home."

Be aware of the room where you sit quietly breathing. Let your consciousness move out as you breathe out, into this space inside the walls, floor, and ceiling that surround you. Feel the roof over your head that is an integral part of the building these walls support. As you breathe in, think, "Home."

Feel the ground that supports this building. The earth that continues miles and miles beneath you, draws you down, supports you as well as this building. As you breathe out, let your consciousness move down into this earth beneath you. Breathing in, think, "Home."

Now feel the open sky above and around you. The blue sky where birds fly, where breezes blow, where this air you breathe comes from. Let your consciousness move out with your breath into this blue sky. Breathing in, think, "Home."

Breathing out, feel the vast open space beyond this blue sky, where the sun and moon circle and shine. Breathing out, let your awareness move out into this vastness, into stars, galaxies, and worlds beyond worlds. Breathing in, be aware that you reside in this vastness, and think, "Home."

Relax in this great openness, breathing in and out, letting your awareness float out and feeling your home as you breathe in.

Now continuing to let your breath flow out into this vast universe, feel that this vastness returns into you, into this ground where you sit, this blue sky over you, this roof, this floor, and this cushion. Breathing in, feel your breath fill your belly, and think, "Home."

The Healing Life of Nature

Medicine and sickness cure each other. All the earth
is medicine. Where do you find yourself?

ZEN MASTER UMMON

The natural world is a spiritual house. . . . Man walks
there through forests of physical things that are also spiritual things, that watch him with affectionate looks.

CHARLES BAUDELAIRE

Depression is a breaking, and breaking open, of our hearts. The agent of that breaking open is the world of self, relationships, and duties—the inescapable realities of human life. As human be-ings we need to be willing to have our hearts broken again and again.

Is that enough for us? Because we also need to find a place where our hearts can be healed over and over again as well. We need a place where we can be refreshed to live in the world again with compassion and action.

We will have periods when we want to close our hearts again—but, once opened up, the heart yearns to remain open for-ever. It can be closed again only through drastic measures, such as deadening ourselves—for example, through drugs, or obsessive work, or compulsive sex.

So where can we find that healing that allows us to remain vulnerable and open, to let our hearts be broken again and again? Meditation and its silence are one place, but there is at least one other. When the world has broken our heart, it is the earth that can heal it again.

Zen literature is rich with references to earth and nature, often as an agent of realization and learning. (When asked who had witnessed his great enlightenment, Buddha reached down and touched the earth.) Most of the world's great religious teachings demonstrate a similar reverence toward the earth. Jesus' teachings, for example, show a tenderness toward trees, plants, and flowers. When Jesus needed healing and teaching for his spirit, he went alone into the wilderness. And when Saint Francis asked a tree to speak to him of God, it burst into flower in the midst of winter.

In depression, we may feel so alone that often we can't bear to leave our room, let alone our house. Yet in the quiet places outside we can find acceptance, love, and healing. The birds do not care if we are depressed, and they do not judge us. If we are quiet and still, they will sit near us and sing to us of hope and beauty, when we are hard-pressed to find either in our life. The earth will support us, and a tree will shelter us. As Buddha said, the rain falls on everyone equally and does not make any distinctions between enlightened and unenlightened. Nor does the sun make distinctions between depression and joy.

To be out in the world in this way can also help us to move beyond ourselves and our pain. We can, perhaps, begin to see and feel the absolute perfection of all things just as they are. If we are quiet, we may even find the answers we need.

When I was deep in my own depression, I spent some time on the shores of Lake Superior. I climbed a low mountain that overlooked the lake. I found an outcropping of rock and sat there in meditation, making a silent prayer. I wasn't even sure what it was I was asking or looking for, but I knew I needed something. I vowed to sit and wait for the answer.

It was the end of October and very cold. After nearly an hour the cold stone beneath me began to penetrate into me, and then it began to snow. I waited a few more minutes and decided that the answer I was looking for was not coming. I gave up and was just ready to stand up.

Then I felt a sudden rush of air. Two ospreys flew just a few feet over my head, so close I could hear their feathers rustling as they cut over the ridge and descended down toward the great lake.

Jesus said to seek and you shall find; ask and it shall be given to you. In the healing life of nature, the answer may come even when you have finally given up seeking.

For me the answer that day was, *Stop running around asking and seeking. Surrender and be quiet, and you will see the miracles that are going on all around you.*

Further Exploration

Walk out of your door and go outside. Whether you go to your own backyard garden, the top of an apartment building in the midst of the city, or the deepest wilderness, notice the life that is all around you. Hear the sounds, whether they are the cooing of the pigeons in the city or the call of the hawk in the wilderness.

Don't shut out these sounds and feelings and sensations. Let them speak to you as a great song, as a conversation in which anyone can take part.

If you can, and there is enough privacy, try sitting in meditation in this spot or another spot outdoors. Don't view the noises and activity swirling around you as annoyances. Instead, let them be the objects of your attention; let them flow through you, in and out of the house that is your self.

When you are finished, bow to them and thank them for their music.

The Value of Uselessness

Hui Tzu said to Chuang Tzu, "I have a big tree named ailanthus. Its trunk is too gnarled and bumpy to apply a measuring line to, its branches too bent and twisty to match up to a compass or square. You could stand it by the road and no carpenter would look at it twice. Your words, too, are big and useless, and so everyone alike spurns them." Chuang Tzu said, "Maybe you've never seen a wildcat or a weasel. It crouches down and hides, watching for something to come along. It leaps and races east and west, not hesitating to go high or low—until it falls into the trap and dies in the net. Now you have this big tree and you're distressed because it's useless. Why don't you plant it in Not-Even-Anything Village, or the field of Broad-and-Boundless, relax and do nothing by its side, or lie down for a free and easy sleep under it? Axes will never shorten its life, and nothing can ever harm it. If there's no use for it, how can it come to grief or pain?"

CHUANG TZU, *FREE AND EASY WANDERING*

Meditation and spiritual practice really are worthless.

DAININ KATAGIRI ROSHI

In depression we may often feel worthless, that nothing we do matters. We feel beaten down and used up, like an old scrap of cloth not even useful as a rag any longer.

Few of the things human beings do are without a purpose. So our feelings of uselessness in depression seem to strike at the very heart of our being human.

A couple of generations back, most communities had a rag man who would come around collecting household rags. I never understood what his purpose was, until I took a papermaking class. I soon learned that those old, torn, dirty bits of cloth, no longer good for anything in the home, still had value.

First, however, they needed to undergo a transformation. Those rags needed first to be broken down. They were shredded and mashed and mixed with water until they were little more than mud. Only then could the miracle begin. In the hands of a master artisan, those rags became the most beautiful papers. They were now fragile, light, and clean.

They kept some of their strength, but now could be torn much more easily. No longer as solid, they let light shine through; in fact, some glowed with a light that seemed to come from within.

Those rags, which were once judged utterly useless, became something valuable, something that could be of use to others. They could bear the thoughts, poetry, and stories of the culture.

What we judge as useless may simply be useful in a way we can't understand. And too often, we confuse usefulness with value.

There can be great value in uselessness. In fact, Buddhist teachers often tell us, to properly practice meditation, we should do it with no thought of gain. We do it simply to do it.

In the midst of our feelings of worthlessness and hopelessness, it can actually be a relief to do something that is not purposeful. In meditation we can take a break from having to do something or become something, and just be.

Ideas of value and utility, of worth and uselessness, are just that—ideas that human beings attach to things in our world. There is a larger world that we can begin to see, a world beyond notions of usefulness and uselessness.

When we give up seeking gain, when we can simply see the truth of *being* rather than *doing,* we may even discover our own real value.

Further Exploration

*Take a day to give up your ideas of usefulness. Give in to the feelings
you may have had of wanting to do nothing, but you held back from.
Do nothing all day, or do only the things you want to—fly a kite,
watch the same movie three times, or lie back and watch clouds float
by all day.*

*Do you feel guilty? Self-indulgent? Are you afraid nothing will get
done or that you will come to like it too much?*

*Can you take pleasure in all of these useless things, pleasure simply
in being? Can you even give up believing this will be good for you and
simply allow yourself to do it?*

---

*A popular saying today has it that we should "commit random acts of
kindness." For one day commit simply random acts. Are there things
that seem foolish to do that you may suddenly want to do? What happens when you actually do them? Is it difficult to do things without
expectation of results or effect?*

Effort

One should practice meditation with the intensity of
someone trying to put out a fire in their hair.

DOGEN

When we are depressed, simply getting up and crossing a
room can seem to require tremendous effort. And though it provides us an opportunity to learn about our constant busyness, and
to begin to see the value of not-doing, even this learning seems to
require an effort from us.

But usually when we even hear the word *effort,* we equate it
with expending energy—with work. In the midst of the physical
exhaustion that comes with depression, just hearing the word *effort*
can make us feel more tired.

But the effort we need in depression is not, at base, a physical one. Rather, it is a commitment, a work of the heart rather than
the body.

Dogen said that it is through meditation practice that we
manifest our enlightenment—indeed, that practice itself *is* enlightenment. The effort involved in doing meditation is different from
what we are accustomed to thinking of as effort. It is not necessarily
a form of pushing or moving toward some goal. Rather it is the effort of simply being present, of showing up for our lives and learning to appreciate them.

Our habits and conditioning are deep. Effort is required for
us to see them as they arise and not to let them run us. To be present
in the midst of our pain, suffering, and doubt in depression requires
effort as well. Now and in the future, we will continue to have pain.

The temptation is to turn this pain into suffering by trying to avoid it—and thus increasing it.

To stand up in the midst of our suffering requires effort. To do what we know the moment requires of us also requires effort. And to simply get through our depression at times requires a great effort.

Where we get confused is in mistaking our own resistance as effort. The effort that is required of us is not like what we need when pushing a car out of a ditch. Instead, it is simply a willingness to be present, to be attentive, and to be compassionate. It is doing things wholeheartedly.

In depression, as in meditation, sleepiness is at least as much of a problem as pain. It was certainly a difficulty for me. For some time I thought of effort in meditation in terms of how to resist sleepiness. That view left me with two ways to deal with the problem. Sometimes I would struggle hard, trying to stay awake. Yet when I did, I would invariably find myself asleep, sometimes pitching forward and nearly falling off my pillow. The other option seemed to be to give in. I would take a balanced posture on my cushion and just sleep for forty minutes until the bell ending meditation rang. Not much meditation went on with either approach.

During one long meditation retreat I was having particular problems with drowsiness, and as usual my two approaches weren't accomplishing much. Finally I realized that, rather than fight or give in to it, there was a third option: I decided to simply watch my sleepiness. It didn't take very long before I was amazed: I no longer was pitching forward like a driver late at night. Nor was I quietly getting forty winks on the cushion. Instead, I felt more alert than I usually did, even when I wasn't sleepy at all. The drowsiness didn't go away. It continued, but when I stopped resisting, it wasn't a problem any longer. It simply became part of all that I was paying attention to.

I made much the same mistake for a long time in my depression. Finally, I discovered that the solution was the same: to stop fighting the depression, *and* to stop consciously surrendering to it. Instead, I simply watched it in all its manifestations. That was when my real healing began.

We create many problems for ourselves in depression through our efforts to beat it back or manage it. But if we instead make an effort to simply be aware, to simply watch it, rather than fighting or giving in to it, we may find the peace, energy, and joy that lie just behind it.

Work

Hyakujo used to labor at his temple even at the age of eighty, trimming the gardens, cleaning the grounds, and pruning the trees. The monks felt sorry to see the old teacher working so hard, but they knew he would not listen to their advice to stop, so they hid away his tools. That day the master did not eat, nor did he eat the following day. The monks finally put his tools back. That day Hyakujo worked and ate, just as he had before. In his evening talk he told them, "No work, no food."

ZEN STORY

A monk said to Joshu, "I have just entered this monastery. Please teach me." "Have you eaten your rice gruel?" asked Joshu. "Yes, I have," replied the monk. "Then you had better wash your bowl," said Joshu. With this the monk gained insight.

MUMONKAN, CASE 7

Depression is characterized by slowness, by inactivity, by an inability to make decisions and carry out actions. There is much to learn from this facet of depression, but there are times when we nevertheless must act.

For activity is important to healing depression. Physical exercise has been shown to be effective in lessening depression. Furthermore, to accomplish something, to be useful, can go a long way toward overcoming our feelings of worthlessness. And the simple fact is that, though there is much to be learned and gained through silence, stillness, and introspection, there is work that we must do to support our lives. Food must be cooked, houses must be cleaned, children must be cared for, clothing must be washed.

We often think of meditation and Zen practice in terms of stillness, of passivity, of not-doing—many of the same characteristics that apply to our depression. Yet in meditation the moment comes when we must get up off the cushion and do something. Even in an intensive Zen meditation retreat, meditation is interwoven with activity—the work of cooking meals, washing dishes, and maintaining the building and grounds.

In traditional Zen monasteries, the job of chief cook was given to a senior monk as part of his or her spiritual practice. More than any other position, the cook's required hard work. It also left little time for meditation. Here we can see Zen's dual emphasis: on activity and work on the one hand, and on silence and stillness on the other.

Like the monks in a Zen monastery, rather than seeing work as only a distasteful necessity, we can consider it part of our spiritual path and practice. We can remain mindful and attentive while going about our activities.

We can also see work as part of our healing process, and afford it the same importance that we attach to anything else we do to that end. Doing the dishes, cleaning the car, or going to our job can be as helpful as anything else we do. It need not be a great accomplishment; just making some effort toward getting up and doing something each day will make a difference, and move us along our path of healing.

We can find the balance in our life between stillness and activity. In doing so, we can begin to live so that all things are opportunities for learning and healing. We can wholly participate in the world with mindfulness and compassion—not just in the (relatively) easy realm of silence and calm, but in the noisy, messy world of human life.

Further Exploration

Bring your attention to some work that needs to be done. Rather than rushing through the task so you can be done with it, bring the same attention to your work that you would to your breathing in meditation.

Perform your work slowly, so that you can do it with full attention. Make your focus the sensations and experience of the work, not the completion of it. Your purpose is the attention you give, not the job that needs to be done.

If you are sweeping the floor, notice the feel of the broom in your hand, the sound of it over the floor, the swirls of dust in its wake. If you are doing dishes, feel the soapy water on the plate, the warmth of the water, your breath in your belly, the weight of your body on the soles of your feet.

When you have finished a task, don't just hurry on to the next thing that needs to be done. Rather notice your breathing. Take a moment to feel the space between your tasks, like the silence between the notes in music.

Parental Mind

> A parent, irrespective of poverty or difficult circumstances,
> loves and raises a child with care. How deep is love like
> this? Only a parent can understand it. A parent protects
> the children from the cold and shades them from the hot
> sun with no concern for his or her own personal welfare.
> Only a person in whom this mind has arisen can under-
> stand it, and only one in whom this attitude has become
> second nature can fully realize it. This is the ultimate in
> being a parent. In this same manner, when you handle
> water, rice, or anything else, you must have the affection-
> ate and caring concern of a parent raising a child.
>
> DOGEN, *INSTRUCTIONS TO THE COOK*

Much has been said in the last few years about finding our
inner child. In depression we have no trouble finding this person
inside us. In fact, in many ways depression is a return to the ways of
a child. We are unable to take care of ourselves. We don't want to eat
well; we want to sleep late; perhaps we want to eat ice cream in the
morning. We don't want to take on the responsibilities of adult-
hood. We are frightened to go out into the world alone. If we have
children, it is difficult to act toward them (or ourselves) in a parental way.

We need a parent to guide us through the depression. We
need to find our own inner adult—what we might call our own
parental mind.

What are the qualities of parental mind?

Parents are patient and see progress in the smallest steps.
Parents practice unconditional love and acceptance. Parents strive

for equanimity, but if they become angry or frustrated, the emotion is short-lived and does not endanger anyone. Their anger is over with quickly and is used as an opportunity to teach and to learn.

Parents are watchful and attentive. Parents are willing to let themselves take a back seat to another. Parents are always aware of impermanence. (And if they aren't, their child is a living reminder.) Parents see that they cannot control but can only attempt to arrange their circumstances as best they can.

Parents speak gently and calmly, even when angry. Parents are willing to admit mistakes and seek reconciliation. Parents are aware of the limitations of their power.

Parents leave room for joy to assert itself at any moment and experience that joy in simple, fleeting pleasures—or take that joy simply in another's presence.

Parents know that sometimes they must take on a role that is bigger than them (or bigger than they think they are). Parents are always ready to learn from any situation or person—even someone much less experienced.

Parents understand that the results of actions are not always immediately visible, and certainly not predictable. And so a parent goes on faith. But the very act of parenting is to have faith—both in this moment and in some kind of a future, whatever that may turn out to be.

Adopting this state of mind while in depression can be extremely helpful, both for ourselves and for others we encounter. Through it we can take better care of ourselves and be more understanding of ourselves. As a result, we can act with greater awareness and compassion toward everyone we come in contact with.

Buddhist teachers often use the term *monkey mind* to describe the constant jumping about of our thoughts. The term makes me think of the books about the monkey Curious George I read to my son. George is like a toddler, bouncing from one experience to the next, always in search of excitement and new experiences. He does not think of the consequences of his actions.

We can all be like Curious George, but we are particularly susceptible to monkey mind when we are in the grip of our depression. And, just as Curious George discovers by the end of each story, we need a firm but loving hand to set us straight, to keep us on track, and to keep us safe and out of trouble.

We can find just such a hand in ourselves when we discover our own parental mind.

Further Exploration

During the course of a day, treat yourself the way you would treat a small child you were taking care of. If you make mistakes, or get confused, or angry, or afraid, consider how you would respond if that child were to do the same thing. Then respond to yourself in that way.

Would you berate a small child, or shame or yell? Or would you speak gently to the child, and act toward them with kindness, patience, and understanding? If the child made a mistake, would you say he is stupid and worthless, or would tell him that mistakes are how we all learn?

Consider your physical needs in the same way. Would you let a child get too little sleep, or eat nothing but sugar, or not have any time to play or relax? Can you give yourself some of the same care and respect?

You also need to set limits with a small child—not allowing him to throw tantrums, or hurt others, or act disrespectfully toward you or anyone else. Do the same for yourself.

Can you be loving with yourself, yet expect that you will keep your promises?

————

Buddha said that each of us should treat other beings as though they were at one time our mothers, or our children. (And if you believe in reincarnation, they once were.)

What does it mean to treat people in your life in such a way? Can you be understanding with difficult people you meet in your life, while still setting limits and saying no? Can you treat the people you love with the kind of respect and gratitude you would have for someone who cared for you, fed you, protected you, and taught you?

How does it feel to act toward others in this way, even to a small degree? How do they respond to it? Is it difficult? Does it get easier as you do it? How does acting in this way affect your depression?

How do you feel when you act toward yourself *in this way? Does it get easier as you do it? How does acting in this way affect your depression?*

Compassion and Action

My religion is kindness.

DALAI LAMA

The knowledge of emptiness gives birth to compassion.

MILAREPA

When we are struggling with depression, kindness and compassion may seem as rare as water in the desert. We are angry, frightened, and judgmental. We scarcely have the energy to extend kindness or compassion to ourselves, much less to others. At the same time we may find it difficult to believe that anyone might offer us any kindness. We feel abandoned by ourselves and by the world.

Still, the capacity for compassion remains within all of us. In fact, the difficulties we are going through in our depression can lead us to a deeper understanding of our life, as well as greater compassion for others and for ourselves.

As we begin to see that life is full of suffering for all beings, we begin to feel that there is already enough suffering in this world. We wonder why we would want to add to that suffering. Our growing awareness that life is impermanent also gives us a greater compassion for others, and for ourselves as well. Compassion thus arises out of our fuller understanding of ourselves and the nature of our relationship to this world.

Depression slows us down and allows us to come in contact with our raw, tender feelings for ourselves and others. If we can become aware of what is happening to us, then the seed of compassion can grow in our life. The natural compassion that is within us can then come forth, to be put into action in our relationships and activities. (And our understanding and compassion must be acted upon; otherwise they are empty realization.)

It is a cliché that we must care for ourselves before we can care for others, but this is especially true in depression. Until we begin to look beyond the feelings of worthlessness and self-hatred we feel in depression, we have great difficulty in acting with love toward others. As we come to see ourselves more fully through awareness and meditation, we can be more forgiving and compassionate to ourselves as well.

In the darkness of depression, it seems we will never see an end to our suffering. It is hard for us to believe we can help ourselves, much less be of any use to someone else. Yet in our depression, service to others becomes even more important for us to practice.

Depression can be a disease of self, where we become so wrapped up in our own suffering that we become focused on little else but ourselves. Looking to see how we may help others can take us out of the small world of self in which we have been living.

Being of help to another human being is also a strong antidote to the feelings of worthlessness we have in our depression. In addition, we gain some perspective through helping others, so that we don't believe we are the only individual in the world who is suffering.

We need not believe we must do great deeds in order to help others. Each kind word or helpful act serves to make the world a kinder place. The ripples that spread from such an act have effects beyond us that we may never know.

We have already been given a way we can be of great value to others. By surviving our depression, we can give kindness, understanding, and hope to others struggling with it. We can talk honestly about our experience and change some of the prejudices people have about it. We can make a difference.

A Buddhist scripture asks, "There is one alone who has come into the world to help others and relieve their suffering. Who is that one?" It can be no one else but you.

Further Exploration

Sitting quietly, breathe in and out, watching your breath.

Feel the breath coming in, giving warmth and nourishment to your heart. As you breathe in, gently turn your attention to yourself. Hold yourself in the warmth of your heart. Silently say to yourself, "May I be free from suffering. May I feel at peace."

Continue to breathe in, and continue to compassionately hold yourself in your heart. As you breathe in, say, "May I be free from suffering," and as you breathe out, "May I feel at peace." Acknowledge the pain you have felt, and continue to extend this love to yourself.

After you have done this for several minutes, think of a loved one who may particularly need your thoughts. Bring them into your heart. Hold their face before you, and as you breathe in, say to them, "May you be free from suffering," and as you breathe out, "May you feel at peace."

Feel the space in your heart for them grow, and feel your wish for them to be healed. Send your loving thoughts to them, feel them in the openness of your heart, and say to them, "May you be free from suffering. May you feel at peace."

When your heart has grown bigger, extend your loving thoughts out further. Hold all the people in your life in your heart, and as you breathe in, say to them, "May you be free from suffering," and as you breathe out, "May you feel at peace." Continue to feel your love and care for them.

Now open your heart to all the suffering in the world, and as you extend that love out infinitely, say, "May all beings be free from suffering. May all beings feel at peace." Remain here, extending your love to yourself and to all suffering beings: "May all beings be free from suffering. May all beings feel at peace."

Living in Vow

Living in vow, silently sitting
Sixty-three years
Plum blossoms begin to bloom.
The jeweled mirror reflects Truth as-it-is.

DAININ KATAGIRI ROSHI

In depression it can be very difficult to keep a promise we made just a few minutes ago, much less to try to keep a vow for any length of time. Or when we do make a vow, we turn it against ourselves. We use it as proof of our worthlessness and weakness if we even think about breaking it. Rather than allowing our promise to be something that helps us and lifts us up, we use it to beat ourselves down.

But when we are depressed, we need our vow more than at any other time. We can use it to help our healing, to make decisions easier, and sometimes even to keep us safe and alive.

Most of us have taken vows at one time or another. We make wedding vows. Or we make promises to ourselves at New Year's, only to see those resolutions fall by the wayside within a few weeks. So though we have taken vows before, we don't much believe in their value, or indeed their power.

We don't believe in the power of vows to change the world or to change ourselves. Perhaps that is because we look at them, if we use them at all, as magic incantations. We utter our vows once, and then we make no further effort to practice them. Of course then they don't accomplish anything for us.

A friend of mine was in a relationship with a wonderful woman. He wanted to be with her forever, but the very thought of making such a commitment frightened him immensely. Then another friend said something very simple to him that changed his fear. His friend suggested he was wrong in thinking of the vow he would make as being forever. Rather, he should see a vow to love this person as a choice and promise that he makes day after day— not as something to say or do once and then be done with. Within a few months of being given this new understanding, my friend married his love.

To make a promise work is to keep your vow as a living thing, nurtured from moment to moment through choice and attention. My Zen teacher, Katagiri Roshi, spoke of "living in vow." Our vow is alive, and we must live within it ourselves moment by moment.

Yet even if we live within our vow, we may still lose sight of it from time to time and may even break our vow. When we do break it, we do not use that fact as an excuse to give up our vow. We make it once more and recommit to this choice we have made.

When we can keep our vow active and alive, we remove some of the struggle we go through when making a decision about how to act. In a sense, we do not need to decide. We let our vow be alive and make the decision for us.

Buddhist practice uses two kinds of vows: prohibitions and positive resolutions. Buddhists have the ten great prohibitory precepts—abstentions that can lead to a more harmonious life. These precepts include not lying, not taking intoxicants, not stealing, and not harming others. Some criticize prohibitions like these or the Ten Commandments of Christian teaching as being too negative.

But people need both kinds of vows. There are actions that are poisonous enough to our world and ourselves that vowing to abstain from them is the most positive thing we can do. Sometimes it is easier to keep from doing something negative than it is to make an effort to carry out positive action. The act of abstaining can lead to a healthier mind and body, which can then lead to positive actions as well.

In depression there are things from which we need to abstain. One of the great prohibitory precepts is to do no harm to anyone. We can extend this to ourselves as well. We can vow that we will not harm ourselves, first of all through injuring or abusing ourselves. We can decide that suicide will not be a choice for us.

We can also vow that we will not harm ourselves by not taking care of ourselves. We can eat good food, get enough sleep. And we can make vows to carry out positive actions for our healing: taking our medication if that is what we have chosen, getting physical exercise, or finding the time for meditation.

If we can make these vows and live them, then we can live through the pain of our depression.

Further Exploration

Choose something you want to do, or something you want to refrain from doing. Choose something that will bring healing to yourself or others.

Put your intention in the form of a vow. Speak this vow out loud, if only to yourself. Each day speak your vow aloud at least once. Nurture your vow as a living thing.

If you are in a difficult situation or having a hard time, you can use this vow to remind yourself of your intention.

If you are not able to keep your vow perfectly, do not use it as a reason to give up. Repeat your vow, keeping it alive. Let it continue to inform your life and your actions.

Further Reading

Depression

Bloomfield, Harold H., M.D., and Peter McWilliams. *How to Heal Depression*. Prelude Press, 1994.

Burns, David, M.D. *Feeling Good: The New Mood Therapy*. Signet, 1980.

Copeland, Mary Ellen. *The Depression Workbook*. New Harbinger Publications, 1992.

Cronkite, Kathy. *On the Edge of Darkness: Conversations About Conquering Depression*. Doubleday, 1994.

Dowling, Colette. *You Mean I Don't Have to Feel This Way? New Help for Depression, Anxiety, and Addiction*. Bantam, 1993.

Goldberg, Ivan K., M.D. *Questions and Answers About Depression and Its Treatment: A Consultation with a Leading Psychiatrist*. Charles Press, 1993.

Huber, Cheri. *Being Present in the Darkness: Using Depression as a Tool for Self-Discovery*. Perigee Books, 1996.

Jamison, Kay Redfield. *An Unquiet Mind: A Memoir of Moods and Madness*. Knopf, 1995.

Nelson, John, and Andrea Nelson, eds. *Sacred Sorrows: Embracing and Transforming Depression*. Tarcher/Putnam, 1996.

Papolos, Demitri, M.D., and Janice Papolos. *Overcoming Depression: The Definitive Resource for Patients and Families Who Live with Depression and Manic-Depression*. Harper Perennial, 1992.

Styron, William. *Darkness Visible: A Memoir of Madness*. Vintage, 1990.

Thorne, Julia, with Larry Rothstein. *You Are Not Alone: Words of Experience and Hope for the Journey Through Depression*. Harper Collins, 1993.

Buddhism and Meditation

Aitken, Robert. *The Dragon Who Never Sleeps: Verses for Zen Buddhist Practice*. Parallax, 1992.

Aitken, Robert. *Taking the Path of Zen*. North Point Press, 1982.

Beck, Charlotte Joko. *Everyday Zen: Love and Work*. HarperSanFrancisco, 1989.

Bercholz, Samuel, and Sherab Chodzin. *Entering the Stream: An Introduction to the Buddha and His Teachings*. Shambhala, 1994.

Boorstein, Sylvia. *Don't Just Do Something, Sit There: A Mindfulness Retreat with Sylvia Boorstein*. HarperSanFrancisco, 1996.

Boorstein, Sylvia. *It's Easier Than You Think: The Buddhist Way to Happiness.* HarperSanFrancisco, 1995.

Braverman, Arthur. *Warrior Zen: The Diamond Hard Wisdom Mind of Suzuki Shosan.* Kodansha, 1994.

Chodron, Pema. *When Things Fall Apart: Heart Advice for Difficult Times.* Shambhala, 1997.

Cleary, Thomas, trans. *The Dhammapada.* Bantam, 1995.

Dogen and Uchiyama. *Refining Your Life: From the Zen Kitchen to Enlightenment.* Weatherhill, 1983.

Goldstein, Joseph. *The Experience of Insight: A Simple and Direct Guide to Buddhist Meditation.* Unity, 1987.

Hagen, Steve. *Buddhism Plain and Simple.* Tuttle, 1997.

Katagiri, Dainin. *Returning to Silence: Zen Practice in Daily Life.* Shambhala, 1988.

Katagiri, Dainin. *You Have to Say Something: Manifesting Zen Insight.* Edited by Steve Hagen. Shambhala, 1998.

Kornfield, Jack. *A Path with Heart: A Guide Through the Perils and Promises of Spiritual Life.* Bantam Doubleday, 1993.

Levine, Stephen. *A Gradual Awakening.* Anchor, 1989.

Levine, Stephen. *Guided Meditations, Explorations, and Healings.* Doubleday, 1991.

Morreale, Dan. *The Complete Guide to Buddhist America.* Shambhala, 1998.

Packer, Toni. *The Work of This Moment.* Tuttle, 1995.

Rahula, Walpola. *What the Buddha Taught.* Grove, 1986.

Reps, Paul. *Zen Flesh, Zen Bones.* Shambhala, 1994.

Salzberg, Sharon. *A Heart As Wide As the World: Living with Mindfulness, Wisdom, and Compassion.* Shambhala, 1997.

Somé, Malidoma Patrice. *Ritual: Power, Healing, and Community.* Swan Raven, 1993.

Suzuki, Shunryu. *Zen Mind, Beginner's Mind.* Weatherhill, 1972.

Tanahashi, Kazuaki, and Tensho David Schneider. *Essential Zen.* HarperSanFrancisco, 1994.

Thich Nhat Hanh. *Being Peace.* Parallax, 1987.

Thich Nhat Hanh. *Living Buddha, Living Christ.* Riverhead, 1997.

Thich Nhat Hanh. *Miracle of Mindfulness: A Manual on Meditation.* Beacon, 1992.

Trungpa, Chogyam. *Cutting Through Spiritual Materialism.* Shambhala, 1987.

Watson, Burton. *Chuang Tsu: Basic Writings.* Columbia University Press, 1964.

Whyte, David. *The Heart Aroused: Poetry and the Preservation of the Soul in Corporate America.* Doubleday, 1994.